southern pies

southern pies

A GRACIOUS PLENTY *of* PIE RECIPES, FROM LEMON CHESS TO CHOCOLATE PECAN

By Nancie McDermott

Photographs By LEIGH BEISCH

CHRONICLE BOOKS
SAN FRANCISCO

DEDICATION To Minister Robert Lee Campbell, chef, poet, and Vietnam veteran; husband and father; deacon, preacher, and teacher; bold, faithful community leader; and peaceful warrior for justice. Thank you for showing that the pie is big enough for all of us to share.

ACKNOWLEDGMENTS What a sweet and glorious abundance of good, brilliant, creative, and generous people I have on my cookbook-cooking-up team! Deepest gratitude and respect to my editor Bill LeBlond, who took a chance on my first book a few miles back along this road. Warmest thanks to Amy Treadwell, Peter Perez, Sarah Billingsley, Anne Donnard, Tera Killip, Doug Ogan, and David Hawk at Chronicle Books, for creativity, energy, smarts, and patience beyond the call. For photographs that are lovely and moving beyond words, all praise and glory to Leigh Beisch and her amazing team. Finally, big sweet Southern hugs to precious friends and family, starting with Lisa Ekus, literary agent as well as dear friend; and to Susanne and Bill Settle, Jill O'Connor, Sandra Gutierrez, Dean Nichols, Debbie Gooch, Connie Gates, Brenda Hines, Lorie Clark, Louise Parrish, Shelbie White, Libbie Hall and Edna Hall Gambling, Kevin Hicks and Suepinda Keith, Stan Cheren, Renny and Bria Johnson, Bob and Vada Satterfield, and my sweeter-than-chess-pie family, Will, Camellia, and Isabelle Lee.

Library of Congress Cataloging-in-Publication Data available.
ISBN 978-0-8118-6992-8

Manufactured in China
Designed by **Anne Donnard**
Prop styling by **Sara Slavin**
Food styling by **Dan Becker**
Typesetting by **Kate Parun**

10 9 8 7 6 5 4 3 2 1

Chronicle Books LLC
680 Second Street
San Francisco, CA 94107
www.chroniclebooks.com

Table of Contents

Introduction

Apple pie may be the quintessential all-American dessert, but like so many sources of national pride and joy, it really is a Southern pie. With Virginia, the Carolinas, and Georgia among the original thirteen colonies, the flourishing roots of modern American culinary tradition run deep, and they tend to lead in a southerly direction. Not that the South has any exclusive claim on the all-American apple pie, but the signature pies of the American South are many and glorious—some born here, some adopted from elsewhere—and all are alive and well and thriving from Tampa to Texas, Charleston to Little Rock, and everywhere in between. This book explores and celebrates the abundance of pies Southern people make and love, and of those, we have a gracious plenty.

Trace pies back to colonial-era Southern kitchens and you will find yourself further transported across the Atlantic Ocean to England, which the first successful colonies still called "home." The earliest references to pie (or rather, "pye") date to thirteenth-century Britain. While such "pyes" tended to be hearty and savory—a main meal rather than a snack or a dessert—by the 1400s, sweet pastries and fruit pies were coming into their own. Claims that Queen Elizabeth I made the first cherry pie are surely an urban (or urbane Elizabethan) legend, but it is quite likely that she consumed sweet pies and tarts at her royal dining table.

Such early pies consisted of a serviceable but often-unappetizing crust—a disposable vessel, or dense and sturdy vehicle—for the filling rather than a tasty component of the actual pie. The name for such vessels in the thirteenth century conveys the lack of culinary emphasis. It was the profoundly unappetizing "coffin," clearly expressing the purpose of the item as a service object rather than a complement to the meal. By the time colonial cooks regularly baked mince, apple, and custard pies in their hearth ovens after the meat and bread were done, the inedible vessel evolved. Cooks had come round to embracing the casing, with edible pastry designed to enhance the pie rather than merely deliver its contents. The name improved, too, with the rather macabre "coffin" giving way to "piecrust" in the colonial culinary parlance.

British influences found colonial Southern cooks baking proper English-style custards, mincemeat, and fruit pies. Over time, these new Americans created their own repertoire, using ingredients available in their gardens and marketplaces. The South's diversity in terms of climate, geography, and agriculture brings much regional color to the pie story. Many pies are common throughout the South, including egg custard pie (page 32), lemon cloud pie (page 15), chess pie (page 50), pecan pie (page 55), and sweet potato pie (page 34). Others reflect their origins by featuring local ingredients. These include Key lime pie (page 106) in South Florida, peanut pie (page 56) in rural Virginia, black walnut pie (page 108) in the Appalachian Mountains, and scuppernong meringue pie (page 68) throughout the Low Country of the coastal Carolinas and Georgia. Southern pies reflect seasonal changes as well, from pies and cobblers made with blackberries, blueberries, and peaches to celebrate summer's bounty, to those of apple, pear, and mincemeat gracing the autumn and holiday tables. Dried peaches tucked into fried pies provide a welcome note of summer's sweetness come winter, and rhubarb stalks point out the arrival of spring (rhubarb is still widely known as "pie plant" in rural areas of the modern South).

Economy played a part in the evolution of a number of old-time pies, too. Southern farm families dried bushels of apples and pears as well as summertime peaches, for use in double-crust pies and fried pies alike. Vinegar Pie (page 47) and Molasses Pie (page 43) stretched pennies while putting everyday homemade ingredients to work. Pies made with saltine crackers (and later Ritz Crackers for the more modern "mock apple pie") also made financial sense and sweetened life nicely with little cost. Also inexpensive and delicious were bean pies (page 39) and Irish potato pies (page 38). Each of these frugal favorites involves stirring the namesake ingredient into a classic custard mixture, yielding a worthy variation on the pumpkin pie–sweet potato pie theme. These heirloom pies remain beloved in the hearts of many a Southerner, including myself, now that I have found my way to them in researching this book.

In addition to classic pies, seasonal pies, regional pies, and economical pies, you'll love the pies created in the kitchens of modern-day chefs and cooks. To show how Southern cooks continue to improvise within their pie-making tradition, you'll find a few exemplary pies from twenty-first-century Southerners. These include Mississippi native Martha Hall Foose's Sweet Tea Pie (page 53), Barry Maiden's Hungry Mother Spicy Peanut Pie (page 56), Nathalie Dupree's Peaches and Cream Pie (page 65), Sandra Gutierrez's Peach-Pecan Pie (page 66), and David Guas's Apple-Pecan Crumble Pie (page 84).

Any way you roll out and fill up their various crusts, Southern pies are alive, well, and thriving in the twenty-first century. They still show up on farmhouse kitchen windowsills and elegant dining room tables; in cafeterias and cafes; on gas station and convenience store counters; in fine restaurants, truck stops, and meat-and-three joints. They star at Juneteenth celebrations, dinners on the grounds, Thanksgiving gatherings, and church homecomings. They disappear at farmers' markets, and many a piece of bake-sale pie has failed to make it home altogether.

Southern pies make the sweetest possible sense here and now. It's never been easier to make them, with ready-to-drape, refrigerated piecrusts that work just fine. Pies belong in every cook's repertoire: They go together fast, and each pie teaches you a skill upon which you can expand into more pies—building on what you already

know. For example, make blackberry cobbler (page 73), and then switch fruits to peaches, blueberries, or strawberry and rhubarb. When you've got apple pie down, do it over with crisp autumn pears. After you get Old-Time Chess Pie (page 48), move on over to the equally simple and nearly irresistible lemon chess or chocolate chess pies. Once you know how to make meringue, you've got it for life. And if meringue is just too much, sweetened whipped cream or ice cream make beautiful and luxurious finishes. In fact, consider topping your pies one option, but not a requirement. My grandmother never topped her pies, other than to put meringue on the ones that she considered in that genre. She thought her chess pies, peach pies, blackberry cobblers, sour cherry pies, mincemeat pies, and the like were all just fine the way she made them, and of course she was right.

You don't have to be Southern to love these pies, to enjoy reading about them, or to get in the kitchen and make them. Anyone from anywhere can learn to how to do it. All you need is the wish to put pie making into your culinary repertoire. The phrase "easy as pie" only rang true to me once I got my hands deeply into the process of writing this book. There's the issue of crust making, and it's something of an art. But it's simple enough to learn it should you be so inclined. If you are not, there are the modern blessings of piecrust in many ready-when-you-are forms, from rolled out and refrigerated to frozen pie shells, and for some pies, graham cracker and cookie crumb crusts. Fillings can be as simple as whisking up eggs, sugar, and milk for a custard pie; or mounding chunks of ripe peaches or an avalanche of fresh berries into an unbaked pie shell and sweetening it up. The possibilities are endless and so are the joys of making, baking, eating, and sharing the treasures within the repertoire of Southern pies.

The Pathway to the Pleasures of Making Southern Pies

If you've ever wondered how the expression "easy as pie!" ever came to indicate simplicity, you are in good company. While most people seem to like eating pie in one form or another, and while many people already enjoy making them, more than a few people out there think that making pies is something that only a trained professional should ever attempt to do. My grandmother and her sisters and neighbors and cousins did not know this. They learned to bake over time as one of their life's tasks, and they did it often, confidently, and well. They didn't consider themselves chefs or bakers—they just got in the kitchen and took care of the business at hand.

Today is a great time to take up the craft of baking, particularly that of making pies. Readily available ingredients, equipment, and resources for learning, the freedom to cook because you want to rather than because you must, the leisure time to explore and develop new skills—all of these advantages are ours, and I'm here to tell you that the task at hand is neither rocket science, brain surgery, nor achieving professional culinary perfection. It's learning, exploring, trying, playing, and more, and the pies in this book are mostly ones that originated in the hands of home cooks over time around the South.

To get you started, here are a few notes on equipment and ingredients that you will want to consider as you bake these pies. Very few tools are crucial. You need a pie pan or two for baking, of course. You need a rolling pin if you want to make piecrust or simply roll it out yourself. You need a few mixing bowls, spoons, and forks, and measuring tools if you want to focus only on fillings. In terms of ingredients, with only a few essentials on hand, you'll be ready to make an amazing number and variety of pies. Most of the ingredients in this book of Southern-rooted pies will be easily found in a supermarket, neighborhood grocery store, farmers' market, or specialty food market, and the remaining items can be ordered easily (see page 156). I've also included a note or two on general pie-making concepts. For the scoop on making and working with piecrusts, from mixing it up to rolling it out, filling it and baking with it, look at Basic Piecrusts, on page 134.

Equipment

If you know much about old-time kitchens, you know that fine pies can come from very simple, very low-tech kitchens. The Southern pie-maker's traditional *batterie de cuisine* is quite small, affordable, and easy to use. I enjoy a number of items that my grandmother did not have, and I would be delighted if you did, too. These are tools to consider, and I encourage you to figure out what you need and want as a work in progress. Your baking equipment will reflect who you are and how you want to bake. Check culinary specialty stores, restaurant supply stores, thrift shops, department stores, estate sales, and the mail-order sources listed in the back of this book (page 156) to find what you need.

NESTED STAINLESS-STEEL MIXING BOWLS

These I use every single day, for an array of cooking tasks beyond baking. I love their weight (or rather lightness), the range of sizes, and the sheer number of them. Spread 'em out, use 'em, wash 'em, and stack 'em back up. They also make perfect "double boiler" setups, since you can rest a bowl on top of a saucepan of very hot water, in order to melt chocolate, make cooked meringue, and do other tasks.

PASTRY BLENDER

This old-time tool is still being made, sturdier these days but essentially the same. It's a U-shaped positioning of parallel wires attached to a handle, with which you press down on chunks of butter, shortening, or lard, and chop them up into coarse bits as you start making pastry dough. You can also do this with two table knives, perfect for "cutting" in the fat, as we say, or your hands, which add heat to the process, but which, if you work fast and with a light touch, can do the job nicely.

FOOD PROCESSOR

This grand machine makes it easy to have great success with making piecrust dough from scratch. If you have one, check the handbook for directions on your particular machine. It's fast, and it's easy to see how the process is going.

ROLLING PINS

My favorite rolling pin is a good-sized wooden dowel, which bulges out in the center and tapers on either end (known as a French pin). I keep it out, where I can get to it anytime. Other materials people love include marble or wooden rolling pins that have separate handles and roll-on bearings. Get a good one and use it a lot, always rolling from the center out, in all four directions.

PASTRY CLOTH

My grandmother had one, which she kept folded up in her main mixing bowl, under her sifter and big wooden spoon. I don't use one now, but I remember it fondly. It kept the crust from sticking to the kitchen table or countertop, and allowed her to lift the crust and move it about without tearing or stretching it. You could accomplish some of that with waxed paper, or you can also find pastry cloth with diameters marked on them, which is helpful.

PLASTIC PASTRY-ROLLING SHEET

You can find heavy-duty plastic pastry sheets now, which do the same job as the pastry cloth. They often have dimensions marked out, so that it is quite easy to see how far along you are in making a pastry circle of a certain dimension.

BAKING PARCHMENT, WAXED PAPER, AND/OR ALUMINUM FOIL

I keep all three of these on hand but I can be excessive in this area. I'm partial to waxed paper, because it's what my grandmother used, and because baking parchment was once rather difficult for me to find. Nowadays it's on the shelf in my supermarket, near the foil and waxed paper. Keep a good supply of one or two of these on hand for rolling out piecrust, using to blind bake a crust, or to help pour sifted dry ingredients.

PIE PANS

Treat yourself to a few good-quality pie pans; one will not be enough if you enjoy making your first few pies, as I deeply hope you will do. My standard go-to pie pan is metal, darkish grey but not extremely dark, and has a standard depth and easy-to-pick-up rim. I also have some ceramic and heatproof glass pie pans. Metal is the great all-purpose pie pan material, though. Heatproof glass allows for excellent browning of the bottom crust, and the opportunity for you to see how that process is going. Ceramic is gorgeous, and holds heat well; the more you bake with a given ceramic pie pan, the better you can gauge the timing. It may take longer than recipes say, depending on its shape and thickness. Use it and you will learn its ways. Ceramic pie pans are also often a larger capacity, excellent if you want to have a deep-dish option in your pie pan collection.

DOUGH SCRAPER

My grandmother did not have a dough scraper, but she would have loved it. I have metal ones with wooden handles, and a sturdy plastic one; it's good to have several. This simple rectangular blade allows you to move pastry about easily, recover sticky piecrust that adheres to your work surface, and clean up the workspace fast once your piecrust is done.

PIE SERVER

My husband got me a pie server when I began work on this book, and I had no idea how useful it would be. While you can use spatulas and butter knives with good results, this peculiar wedge-shaped tool gives you maximum precision and flexibility in removing pieces of pie from the pan, serving it, and keeping the crust intact. Gravity and a less-than-steady hand are against you; this tool gives you the upper hand in getting your pie from pan to plate.

CRUST SHIELD

See "A Few General Tips" (at right) for notes on this piece of equipment.

WHISK OR EGGBEATER

I have both of these tools, and a big balloon whisk is grand for making quick work of simple fillings. The manual eggbeater takes me back, and makes wonderful old-time sounds. I also find great success in using a good-sized table fork for a lot of the mixing and stirring of simple old-school pies. Many of them are just that easy.

WOODEN SPOON AND SPATULA

I keep both of these handy, right by the stove. They are indispensable for stirring fillings without transferring heat to your hand.

ENORMOUS CANISTERS

If you love to bake or think you might, having easy access to generous amounts of flour and sugar is a great gift to yourself. Pastry kitchens have big bins on wheels; you don't need that much, but an oversized jar with a mouth wide enough for you to reach in and scoop with ease is a pleasure indeed. You can keep ten or fifteen pounds of flour and sugar handy, a scoop away from your next pie.

A Few General Tips

FILLINGS BOILING OVER IN THE OVEN

To avoid the difficulties of pies boiling over as they bake, consider placing double-crust pies with fruit fillings, or pies in the chess family with lots of sugar, eggs, and butter on a baking sheet before you place them in the oven to bake. You could also place a sheet of aluminum foil or a baking sheet on the floor of the oven below the baking pie, to make clean up easier should something occur in the bubbling up department.

OVERBROWNING OF PIECRUST EDGES

No matter how careful you are, the issue of the top crust getting nice and brown and done in advance of the rest of the pie being ready is one that remains part of my pie-making world. You can do three things about this challenge. First, you can fashion a wreath of protection out of aluminum foil. Tear off two strips, each about three inches wide and the length of the roll. Lay them shiny-side down, with short ends overlapping each other. Fold, pinch, and press the two ends together one way or another, so that you have one long strip of foil. Pick up this strip, join the loose ends together, and pinch them as before, so that you have a wreath of foil just covering the outer crust edges. Place this loosely over the raw or partially baked crust of your pie, before it goes into the oven. Bake the pie about halfway through its oven time, and then carefully remove the foil wreath. The crust should brown nicely in the remaining time. Second, you can purchase a piecrust shield, a flat wreath of lightweight metal, about ten inches in diameter.

It is a permanent reusable version of the ring of foil previously described and can be found in baking supply stores or ordered from vendors, including the Pampered Chef. It's handy, easy to store under your pie pans, and it does the job well. Third, you can let the oven and the piecrust do what they will do, and simply cut away and discard the overly browned or burned crust once you're ready to serve the pie. If your pie then looks less lovely than you would like, consider dolloping sweetened whipped cream around the rim of the pie, making a luxuriously tempting alternative crust. I've done all these things, and they've served me well.

STORING PIES

To store the pies in this book, follow basic food-safety guidelines. Keep hot things hot, cold things cold, and beware the zone in-between the two (40 to 140 degrees F), at which food begins to spoil. Pies that are to be served warm or at room temperature can sit out on the counter to cool down if you're close to serving time. If you've made such a pie in advance, cover it and refrigerate it until an hour or two before serving time. Let it come to room temperature slowly for best flavor and texture. For pies that are baked in the oven but served cold, let them cool down completely at room temperature; cover and refrigerate until just before serving time. For pies that are stirred together and served cold, such as Key Lime Pie (page 106), cover and refrigerate as soon as you finish making them, and serve very cold. For leftover pie, whether you plan to serve it cold or not, cover it well and refrigerate until near serving time.

PATCHING HOLES

If you've made a piecrust and baked it in advance, you may end up with holes or cracks. If the pie will be filled and baked, you can patch any holes with more pastry dough, which will cook along with the filling. If you'll be filling the baked pastry crust with a cold filling, you could place a crust of bread or a little batch of soft bread crumbs or cracker crumbs completely over the hole or opening. The filling will cover and soften the addition, and when you cut the pie, all will be well.

MERINGUE ANXIETY

As a pie lover from my earliest childhood days, I have always adored any and all pies with meringue on top. To me, the beauty they promise is fulfilled in the celestial pleasures they deliver in flavor and texture. I read lots of advice in baking literature, aimed at resolving what seem to be terrible problems involving meringue. These include how to avoid "weeping" meringue, the small golden beads that sometimes form on the surface. They address the issue of shrinkage between the crust edge and the pie's meringue crown. They advise on handling the syrup that sometimes forms between meringue and filling. They strongly suggest no one attempt meringue making on a humid day. I have had all these things happen in the course of my meringue-making years—which are many, as I've cooked since about age ten. None of them strikes me as tragic or even very worrisome; in fact I adore the little golden beads and wish I knew exactly how to create them, not to avoid them. If there are cracks and gaps, they are usually small; if there is a clear syrup between meringue and filling, it is sweet and delicious and could be considered a bonus sauce. What with air conditioning in so many of today's kitchens affecting the temperature and humidity, and the countless ways that things can and will go wrong no matter what we do in cooking as in life, I say, "Take it easy!" and advise learning your way around meringue making by doing it often and enjoying the results. As the saying goes, perfection is the enemy of the good; unless you burn your meringue, or filling, or lattice-topped crust to smoking cinders, or drop the pie facedown on the floor, you will very likely have something you can still eat. Don't worry. Enjoy cooking. Love the meringue you make, and share it with somebody who could use some pie.

ANTIQUES and HEIRLOOMS

MRS. NATHA ADKINS PARKER'S
LEMON CLOUD PIE 15

CHEF BURTON'S NEW ORLEANS LEMON PIE 16

PINEAPPLE-COCONUT PIE 18

COCONUT CUSTARD PIE 19

COCONUT CREAM PIE 21

AMAZING COCONUT PIE 23

JAPANESE FRUIT PIE 24

DAMSON PLUM CUSTARD PIE 25

BUTTERSCOTCH PIE 27

L ooking back to the Southern kitchens where wood fired the cooking and eating what was fresh and in season was a required rather than a chosen path, two ingredients stand right up and wave real hard. Lemon is one and coconut is the other. Both are dramatic, extraordinary, and multifaceted as ingredients in the kitchen, then and now. Each has its unique qualities: lemon its aromas, colors, extreme flavor, and tendency to move in and take over any dish. Coconut has glamour and a breathtaking beauty at its heart—one all the more precious for the serious slog of effort and mess that it takes a cook to get inside the nut. What it lacks in color, it more than surpasses in charm and substance. Coconut is richness, beauty, delicacy of lace, and lusciousness of velvet and cream. Shredded, flaked, toasted, sprinkled, or stirred into a custard or paired with nuts and raisins in a cookie or an icing, coconut says, "Showtime!" and catches our eyes and appetites.

Neither is native to the Southern landscape, though certainly lemon trees can be found in Florida's more tropical areas. No doubt the keeping qualities of both of these ingredients gave each one time to earn a following in the kitchens and at the Southern table. Before refrigeration was common, boatloads of coconuts, lemons, and tropical fruits like pineapple would arrive at Southern ports from faraway shores, and end up in the marketplace in time to be enjoyed without spoiling. They wouldn't have been common, even in wealthy homes, but that only increased the pleasure and luxury that lemon and coconut conveyed.

There are two more old-timers worthy of a modern family reunion. Damson plum pie uses damson plum jelly for a tart sweet touch and, like butterscotch pie, comes with a delectably delicious crown of meringue.

Let this chapter remind you of old-fashioned celebrations where a few simple ingredients married with lemon or coconut, brown sugar, or last summer's jam can become a memorable dessert—a culinary antique that still suits us, still gives pleasure, and still works.

Lemon Cloud Pie

MAKES ONE 9-INCH PIE

This lovely lemon pie comes from a marvelous book called *The Lost Art of Scratch Cooking: Recipes from the Kitchen of Mrs. Natha Adkins Parker*. If you enjoy cooking and stories of family connection, you will love and use this book as much as I do. Mrs. Parker raised her family in Stello, Mississippi, and one of her sons, Curtis Parker, realized that her lifetime of culinary knowledge and wisdom was a treasure. He documented her gift for "scratch cooking," presenting it in book form so that we can learn the good old ways and put them to use in our twenty-first-century kitchens. Mrs. Parker calls this simply "Old-Fashioned Lemon Pie," but given its combination of delicate texture and intense flavor, I like to call it "Mrs. Natha Adkins Parker's Lemon Cloud Pie."

PASTRY FOR A 9-INCH SINGLE-CRUST PIE (STORE-BOUGHT OR SEE BASIC PIECRUSTS, PAGE 134)

1 CUP SUGAR

2 TABLESPOONS FLOUR

1½ CUPS MILK

2 TABLESPOONS FRESHLY SQUEEZED LEMON JUICE

2 TABLESPOONS BUTTER, MELTED

1 TABLESPOON GRATED LEMON RIND OR ZEST

2 EGG YOLKS, BEATEN WELL

2 EGG WHITES

Heat the oven to 450 degrees F. Line a 9-inch pie pan with crust and then crimp the edges decoratively (see page 138). Refrigerate it until needed.

In a medium bowl, combine the sugar and flour and use a fork or a whisk to stir them together well. Add the milk, lemon juice, butter, and lemon rind. Stir to mix everything together. Add the egg yolks and stir well.

In another medium bowl, beat the egg whites until they swell up into thick, puffy white clouds, which hold their shape in soft peaks.

Using a spatula or a large wooden spoon, fold the egg whites gently into the lemon filling, scooping and lifting to combine the two mixtures evenly. Pour the filling into the piecrust.

Place the pie on the bottom rack of the oven, and bake for 10 minutes. Reduce the heat to 350 degrees F, and bake until the filling is fairly firm, dry, and puffed up, 20 to 25 minutes more. Place the pie on a cooling rack or a folded kitchen towel and let cool to room temperature.

New Orleans Lemon Pie

MAKES ONE 9-INCH PIE

In a lifetime of professional cooking in the food-driven city of New Orleans, Chef Nathaniel Burton mastered the complex dishes for which the city is world famous. As coauthor, with Dr. Rudy Lombard, of *Creole Feast: 15 Master Chefs of New Orleans Reveal Their Secrets,* Chef Burton presents a who's who of culinary artisans commanding the stoves of New Orleans in the 1980s. This cool, plush lemon confection is simpler than most of Chef Burton's daily creations, simple enough for everyday cooks in search of a doable grand finale. Chef Burton used a baked pastry crust, but I prefer a graham cracker crust.

ONE 9-INCH GRAHAM CRACKER CRUST (STORE-BOUGHT OR SEE PAGE 146)

I CUP SUGAR

2 TABLESPOONS CORNSTARCH

I CUP HALF-AND-HALF

4 EGG YOLKS

I TABLESPOON GRATED LEMON RIND OR ZEST

2 TEASPOONS UNFLAVORED GELATIN

I½ CUPS HEAVY CREAM

¼ CUP FRESHLY SQUEEZED LEMON JUICE

Line a 9-inch pie pan with crust and pinch the edges to form a lip. Bake the crust as directed in the recipe.

In a saucepan or the base of a double boiler, bring about 3 inches of water to a gentle boil. In a heatproof metal bowl or the top of a double boiler, combine the sugar and cornstarch, using a whisk or a fork to mix them well. Add the half-and-half, egg yolks, and lemon rind and stir well.

Place the container over the water and adjust the heat to maintain a lively simmer. Stir with a whisk or large spoon until the filling is very warm. Stir in the unflavored gelatin and cook, stirring often, until the mixture thickens to the texture of very thick cream. Remove from the heat and set aside. Allow the mixture to cool to room temperature, and then cover and refrigerate until the mixture is very cold.

Using an electric mixer or a whisk, whip the cream until it is very thick and holds fairly firm peaks. Add the whipped cream and lemon juice to the filling, and fold gently to combine everything evenly and well. Pile the lemon filling into the pie shell and refrigerate until very cold and firm, about 3 hours. Serve cold.

Pineapple-Coconut Pie

MAKES ONE 9-INCH PIE

I adore this pie, with its combination of two tropical ingredients that have been at home on the Southern pantry shelf for more than a century. Egg custard pie was everyday fare, but with small cans of coconut and crushed pineapple, any cook could elevate the sweet standby to tropical heights. Fresh pineapple and coconut are worth the effort of preparing them for many recipes, but for this pie, enjoy the time-honored shortcuts-in-a-can. No need for adornment here, but a dollop of whipped cream could make for a heavenly enhancement.

PASTRY FOR A 9-INCH SINGLE-CRUST PIE (STORE-BOUGHT OR SEE BASIC PIECRUSTS, PAGE 134)

1 CUP SUGAR

2 TABLESPOONS FLOUR

¼ TEASPOON SALT

½ CUP EVAPORATED MILK, HALF-AND-HALF, OR MILK

2 EGGS, BEATEN WELL

¼ CUP BUTTER, MELTED

1 CUP DRAINED CRUSHED PINEAPPLE

1 CUP SHREDDED OR FLAKED COCONUT, SWEETENED OR UNSWEETENED

Heat the oven to 350 degrees F. Line a 9-inch pie pan with crust and then crimp the edges decoratively (see page 138).

In a small bowl, combine the sugar, flour, and salt and stir with a fork to mix well.

In a medium bowl, whisk together the milk, eggs, and butter. Add the sugar mixture and stir well to dissolve the sugar and combine everything evenly. Add the pineapple and coconut and stir with a large spoon to combine everything into a thick filling. Pour it into the piecrust.

Place the pie on the bottom shelf of the oven. Bake until the filling is firm and puffed, and the crust and filling are golden brown, 35 to 45 minutes. Place the pie on a cooling rack or on a folded kitchen towel and let cool to room temperature.

Coconut Custard Pie

MAKES ONE 9-INCH PIE

This is a grand old pie, as appealing today as it must have been on dining tables in the late nineteenth century. Typically referred to simply as "coconut pie" by Southerners, it provides a luxurious dessert that is simple to prepare. Older recipes offer advice on cracking and grating a fresh coconut, and often include generous gratings of nutmeg—a touch I like very much. Meringue as a finishing touch or stiffly beaten egg whites added to the filling mark older recipes as well. The constants are eggs, sugar, butter, and coconut. Freshly grated coconut is the gold standard, but shredded or flaked coconut makes a wonderful pie.

PASTRY FOR A 9-INCH SINGLE-CRUST PIE (STORE-BOUGHT OR SEE BASIC PIECRUSTS, PAGE 134)

I CUP SUGAR

I TABLESPOON FLOUR

¼ TEASPOON SALT

¾ CUP WHOLE MILK

½ CUP BUTTER, MELTED

3 EGGS, BEATEN WELL

I TEASPOON VANILLA EXTRACT

I CUP SHREDDED OR FLAKED COCONUT, SWEETENED OR UNSWEETENED

Heat the oven to 325 degrees F. Line a 9-inch pie pan with crust and then crimp the edges decoratively (see page 138).

In a medium bowl, combine the sugar, flour, and salt, and stir with a whisk or a fork to combine them well. Add the milk, butter, eggs, and vanilla, and stir to combine everything evenly and well. Stir in the coconut, and mix well. Pour the filling into the piecrust.

Place the pie on the bottom rack of the oven and bake until the filling is firm, dry, puffing up and golden brown, 45 to 55 minutes. Place the pie on a cooling rack or a folded kitchen towel and let cool to room temperature.

Coconut Cream Pie

MAKES ONE 9-INCH PIE

This cool, rich pie is beautiful and incomparably delicious; it stands out among the many luscious sweets you might find on a Southern table when great cooks are aiming to please. The cream pie filling is simple to make once you've done it a few times. Then you will be ready to make another Southern favorite, banana cream pie, using the same velvety custard as the foundation. An elegant meringue cloud is the classic finish, with a little extra coconut sprinkled atop the meringue before baking, to communicate exactly what kind of pie pleasure awaits the lucky ones anticipating a piece.

PASTRY FOR A 9-INCH SINGLE-CRUST PIE (STORE-BOUGHT OR SEE BASIC PIECRUSTS, PAGE 134)

FILLING
¾ CUP SUGAR
⅓ CUP CORNSTARCH

⅛ TEASPOON SALT
3 EGG YOLKS
2¼ CUPS MILK
1¼ CUPS SHREDDED OR FLAKED COCONUT, SWEETENED OR UNSWEETENED

3 TABLESPOONS BUTTER
1 TEASPOON VANILLA EXTRACT

MERINGUE
3 EGG WHITES
5 TABLESPOONS SUGAR

Line a 9-inch pie pan with crust and then crimp the edges decoratively (see page 138). Line and partially bake the crust (see page 139). Let it cool to room temperature.

To make the filling: Combine the sugar, cornstarch, and salt in a small bowl, and use a fork or a whisk to mix them well. In another small bowl, beat the egg yolks.

In a medium saucepan over medium heat, bring the milk almost to a boil, stirring it as it heats up and begins to steam. Scoop out about ½ cup of the hot milk, and pour it into the small bowl of beaten egg yolks, stirring well as you pour. This warms up the eggs and discourages them from curdling when they are cooked. Scrape the warmed egg yolks into the hot milk mixture on the stove and stir well.

Add the sugar-cornstarch mixture to the warm egg-and-milk mixture, and stir well to dissolve it. Continue to cook over medium heat, stirring all the while, until the mixture has thickened to about the consistency of cream and become very smooth and evenly combined. Cook for about 1 minute more, and then remove the pan from the heat.

Add 1 cup of the coconut, the butter, and vanilla. Stir to mix everything together well and until the butter has melted. Place a sheet of plastic wrap directly onto the surface of the filling, and set it aside to cool to room temperature. When the filling has cooled down, pour it into the piecrust and set aside.

(continued)

To make the meringue: Heat the oven to 350 degrees F. Beat the egg whites in a medium bowl with an electric mixer on medium speed until foamy. Increase the speed to high, and add the sugar gradually, about 2 tablespoons at a time. Beat the egg whites until they thicken and swell up into plump, shiny, soft clouds that will hold firm, curly peaks.

Scoop the meringue onto the filling, and spread it out to seal the edges to the crust. Mound it up in the middle, and sprinkle the reserved coconut over the top of the meringue. Place the pie on the middle rack of the oven and bake until the meringue is a beautiful golden brown, 10 to 15 minutes. Place the pie on a cooling rack or a folded kitchen towel and let cool to room temperature, or refrigerate and serve chilled.

Amazing Coconut Pie

MAKES ONE 9-INCH PIE

Also known as "Impossible Pie" because this mixture makes a coconut custard pie that creates its own "crust," this dessert is one to make when you want a homemade treat with minimal effort. A glass pie pan is ideal, if you have one, because it gives the coconut custard the opportunity to develop a delicious golden crust in minimal time.

1½ CUPS SUGAR

½ CUP ALL-PURPOSE FLOUR

2 CUPS MILK

½ CUP BUTTER, MELTED

3 EGGS, BEATEN WELL

1 TEASPOON VANILLA EXTRACT

2 CUPS SHREDDED COCONUT, SWEETENED OR UNSWEETENED

Heat the oven to 350 degrees F. Lightly grease a 9-inch pie pan, using butter or vegetable oil.

In a medium bowl, combine the sugar and flour and use a fork or a whisk to mix them together well.

Add the milk, butter, eggs, and vanilla and stir to mix everything together evenly and well. Stir in the coconut. Pour the filling into the pie pan.

Place the pie on the bottom rack of the oven and bake until fairly firm throughout, puffed, and golden brown, 35 to 45 minutes. Place the pie on a cooling rack or a folded kitchen towel and let cool to room temperature.

Japanese Fruit Pie

MAKES ONE 9-INCH PIE

Southern cooks who remember the cake known as Japanese fruitcake will have a head start on figuring out this old-time pie. A special-occasion pie, this sweet concoction boasts a crunchy top with velvety rich filling underneath. Like its cousin, Japanese fruitcake, Japanese fruit pie has no connection to things Japanese; in fact, its Southern essence is clear in its use of raisins, pecans, and shredded coconut, all standard ingredients in the Southern pantry for centuries. Most likely, whoever named it sought to convey that this pie is unusual, unique, and exceptionally good.

PASTRY FOR A 9-INCH SINGLE-CRUST PIE (STORE-BOUGHT OR SEE BASIC PIECRUSTS, PAGE 134)

I CUP SUGAR

½ CUP BUTTER, MELTED

2 EGGS, BEATEN WELL

I TABLESPOON APPLE CIDER VINEGAR OR WHITE VINEGAR

I TEASPOON VANILLA EXTRACT

½ CUP SHREDDED COCONUT, SWEETENED OR UNSWEETENED

½ CUP RAISINS

½ CUP (ABOUT 2 OUNCES) CHOPPED PECANS

Heat the oven to 350 degrees F. Line a 9-inch pie pan with crust and then crimp the edges decoratively.

In a medium bowl, combine the sugar, butter, eggs, vinegar, and vanilla. Use a whisk or a large spoon to combine everything evenly and well. Add the coconut, raisins, and pecans. Using a large spoon or a spatula, stir well to mix everything into a thick, chunky filling. Pour into the piecrust.

Place the pie on the bottom rack of the oven. Bake until the filling is fairly firm, puffing up, and lightly browned, 30 to 40 minutes. Place the pie on a cooling rack or a folded kitchen towel and let cool to room temperature.

Damson Plum Custard Pie

MAKES ONE 9-INCH PIE

Damsons are small, deep blue, deliciously tart plums that thrive in Southern soil. Faithfully cooked into pies when fresh and in season, damsons have traditionally been a great favorite for putting up in the form of jelly, jam, and preserves. My friend Martha Hall Foose shared this old-time recipe from her Great Aunt Carrye in Pickens, Mississippi. It makes a beautiful pie that is well worth sharing. Martha says that if you can't find damson plum jelly, just use any tart seedless jam or jelly. As author of *Screen Doors and Sweet Tea: Recipes and Tales from a Southern Cook*, Miss Martha knows whereof she speaks.

PASTRY FOR A 9-INCH SINGLE-CRUST PIE (STORE-BOUGHT OR SEE BASIC PIECRUSTS, PAGE 134)

FILLING
¾ CUP SUGAR

¼ CUP BUTTER, SOFTENED

½ CUP DAMSON PLUM JELLY (SEE SOURCES, PAGE 156), OR ANOTHER JELLY OR SEEDLESS JAM

½ CUP EVAPORATED MILK OR HALF-AND-HALF

2 TABLESPOONS FLOUR

I TEASPOON VANILLA EXTRACT

½ TEASPOON SALT

2 EGG YOLKS (SAVE THE 2 EGG WHITES FOR MERINGUE)

I EGG

MERINGUE
2 EGG WHITES

4 TABLESPOONS SUGAR

Heat the oven to 350 degrees F. Line a 9-inch pie pan with crust and then crimp the edges decoratively (see page 138).

To make the filling: In a medium bowl, whisk together the sugar and butter. Add the jelly, milk, flour, vanilla, and salt and stir well.

In a small bowl, combine the egg yolks and whole egg and beat with a fork to mix them well. Add the eggs to the filling and stir to combine everything evenly and well to make a smooth, thick filling. Pour into the piecrust.

Place the pie on the bottom shelf of the oven. Bake until fairly firm, about 25 minutes. Place the pie on a cooling rack or a folded kitchen towel and leave the oven on.

To make the meringue: Beat the egg whites in a medium bowl with an electric mixer on medium speed until foamy. Increase the speed to high, and add the sugar gradually, about 2 tablespoons at a time. Beat the egg whites until they are thick and shiny, and will hold firm, curly peaks. Scoop the meringue onto the damson plum custard, spreading it out to seal the edges to the crust. Mound it up in the middle. Use the back of a spoon to swirl it into curly shapes.

Place the pie on the middle rack of the oven. Bake until the meringue is lightly browned, 12 to 15 minutes. Place the pie on a cooling rack or a folded kitchen towel and let cool to room temperature.

Butterscotch Pie

MAKES ONE 9-INCH PIE

Among the many irresistible dishes for which my dear friend Maxine Nichols is famous, her butterscotch pie stands out. Its handsome color, silky texture, and plush flavor make me afraid to be alone in a room with it, for fear I would eat the whole thing by myself. This is my version of her pie, and it is worthy of adding to your Southern dessert repertoire. Jean Anderson, highly decorated author of countless cookbooks, traces the origins of this butterscotch pie to 1915 in *The American Century Cookbook: The Most Popular Recipes of the 20th Century*, a delicious read and fascinating reference for cooks and food-lovers alike. This recipe calls for a baked piecrust, so plan ahead.

PASTRY FOR A 9-INCH SINGLE-CRUST PIE (STORE-BOUGHT OR SEE BASIC PIECRUSTS, PAGE 134)

FILLING
I CUP PACKED LIGHT OR DARK BROWN SUGAR

⅓ CUP ALL-PURPOSE FLOUR

¼ TEASPOON SALT

1¼ CUPS EVAPORATED MILK, HALF-AND-HALF, OR MILK

3 EGG YOLKS, BEATEN WELL

¼ CUP BUTTER

I TEASPOON VANILLA EXTRACT

MERINGUE
3 EGG WHITES

3 TABLESPOONS SUGAR

Line a 9-inch pie pan with crust and then crimp the edges decoratively (see page 138). Line and fully bake the crust (see page 139).

To make the filling: In a medium saucepan, combine the sugar, flour, and salt. Use a fork or a whisk to mix them together. Add the milk to the saucepan, and cook over medium heat, stirring often, until you have a thickened, smooth sauce, about 10 minutes.

Place the egg yolks in a small bowl. Add about ¼ cup of the hot milk mixture to the egg yolks, stirring constantly as you pour the milk slowly into the bowl. Mix well. Pour the warmed egg yolks into the saucepan of sugar and milk, stirring constantly to help them mix in smoothly.

Cook, stirring often, 2 to 3 minutes more, until the filling is thick and smooth. Remove it from the heat and stir in the butter and vanilla, mixing everything evenly and well. Pour the filling into the baked piecrust and set aside.

To make the meringue: Heat the oven to 350 degrees F. Beat the egg whites in a medium bowl with an electric mixer on medium speed until foamy. Increase the speed to high, and add the sugar gradually, about 1 tablespoon at a time. Beat the egg whites until the meringue is thick, shiny, and able to hold curly firm peaks. Scoop the meringue onto the filling. Spread it out to seal the edges to the crust, mounding it up in the middle. Use the back of a spoon to swirl it up into curly shapes.

Place the pie on the middle rack of the oven. Bake until the meringue has turned a beautiful golden brown, 10 to 15 minutes. Place the pie on a cooling rack or a folded kitchen towel and let it cool. Serve at room temperature, or refrigerate and serve chilled.

BUTTERMILK, SWEET POTATO, and OTHER OLD-SCHOOL CUSTARD PIES

Glance through historical cookbooks, and you'll see that from colonial times forward, there were more meat pies than sweet for the first century, and that what sweet pies there were had a common base: custard. This makes sense, given that the essential ingredients for custard pies—eggs, milk, and sugar, with a dash of vanilla or nutmeg and a simple single pastry crust made of flour and lard—were all within the reach of many a comfortable Southern family. The milk and eggs could be obtained by tending a cow and some chickens, and the flour, sugar, and fat could be bought or traded fairly easily with access to a town of any size.

Custard pies are among my great favorites, partly because they are the first ones I ever made, and they came out just fine. I'm also wildly fond of sweet potato and pumpkin pies, which, at the end of the day, come down to custard pie with a twist. I love the Southern-ism of calling custard "egg custard," as though we need to distinguish it from some other essential ingredient. Since using no egg would mean no custard, I consider it a charming example of Southern excess and wouldn't change it for anything.

Researching Southern pies got me reacquainted with two custard pies I'd nearly forgotten: Buttermilk Pie (page 33) and Bean Pie (page 39). Buttermilk was already fading from mainstream usage by the time I came along, and Bean Pie was one I had only enjoyed at farmers' markets and bakeries run by the Nation of Islam in the 1980s. Both were fabulous, easy to make, and worthy of being known and shared at everyday or special-occasion meals. The almond custard and Irish potato pies (see pages 30 and 38) are so old-school that they scarcely appear in books, but each deserves to enter the new school of Twenty-First-Century Easy-as-Pie Pies.

If you enjoy these types of pies as I do, be thinking about inspirations of your own. Butternut squash makes a marvelous pie, and I've imagined that the sweet and squat kabocha squash would make a magnificent custard pie. Let me know if you get to it before I do—I think it's an idea whose time has come.

STEPHEN SCHMIDT'S

Almond Custard Pie

MAKES ONE 9-INCH PIE

I learned this recipe from my friend, food historian and cookbook author Stephen Schmidt, who calls it "sublime—like marzipan in a crust!" He's right, and as one who explores food history not just in libraries, but in the kitchen, he should know. A prolific writer and dedicated and excellent teacher, he does the detective work that enlivens the past and enhances the present, deliciously. He shared this recipe for a wonderful custard pie made with finely ground almonds and butter, and flavored with rose water, a much-loved addition in the colonial era. To include that essence, which connects early American cooking through medieval Europe to the sweet kitchens of the Middle East, see page 156 for ordering information. Stephen notes that pouring the filling into a heated crust, which has just come from its advance baking in the oven, makes for the best pie. He also suggests that you enjoy this pie the day you make it for the most pleasing results. If grinding up almonds in a food processor presents a problem, you can make a lovely version using commercial almond paste in place of the almonds, melted butter, and most of the sugar; add about ¼ cup of sugar in addition to the almond paste.

PASTRY FOR A 9-INCH SINGLE-CRUST PIE (STORE-BOUGHT OR SEE BASIC PIECRUSTS, PAGE 134)

2 CUPS (ABOUT 8 OUNCES) BLANCHED, SLIVERED ALMONDS

I CUP BUTTER, MELTED

I CUP SUGAR

4 EGGS

I TABLESPOON ALMOND EXTRACT

I TABLESPOON ROSE WATER (OPTIONAL; SEE SOURCES, PAGE 156)

½ TEASPOON SALT

Heat the oven to 350 degrees F. Line a 9-inch pie pan with crust and then crimp the edges decoratively (see page 138). Line and partially bake the crust (see page 139). Cover the crust with a kitchen towel to keep it as warm as possible. Increase the oven temperature to 400 degrees F.

In a food processor, grind the almonds to a fine, dry powder, pulsing on and off and scraping the sides and corners of the work bowl to avoid grinding them to a sticky, oily paste. Set aside.

In a medium bowl, combine the melted butter and the sugar. Using a wooden spoon or a spatula, stir well so that they are thoroughly and evenly mixed together. Add the eggs, one at a time, beating each egg in completely before you add the next one. Add the ground almonds, almond extract, rose water (if you are using it), and salt, and stir to combine everything evenly and well.

Pour the thick, nubby filling into the partially baked crust, and place it on the middle rack of the oven. Bake until the edges puff up and the center is fairly firm, wiggling only a little when you gently nudge the pan, 30 to 40 minutes. Place the pie on a cooling rack or a folded kitchen towel and let cool for at least 20 minutes. Serve warm or at room temperature, ideally the day the pie is made.

Egg Custard Pie

MAKES ONE 9-INCH PIE

The first pie I ever made, egg custard remains one of my great favorites. Simple, satisfying, and lovely to the eye, it can be traced back to the English colonial kitchen. The sugar then came in a massive cone, from which it was chipped off and ground down to powdery grains. Perfect for baking in the remaining gentle heat of a hearthside oven after the bread and roasts came out, egg custard is the anytime, everyday sweet that earns its place with every generation. Not only do I love its history, I cherish the name egg custard, a redundant one that is uttered by Southerners as one word to this day. It is provided at cafeterias and on family reunion dessert tables, not as an afterthought, but as a forethought—a culinary "given" that is sure to please and, for the cook, truly easy as pie. Nutmeg sprinkled over the top before baking provides a beautiful homespun finish. This pie begins with scalded milk—brought within range of a boil but stopped short of it.

PASTRY FOR A 9-INCH SINGLE-CRUST PIE (STORE-BOUGHT OR SEE BASIC PIECRUSTS, PAGE 134)

1¼ CUPS MILK

4 EGGS

¾ CUP SUGAR

I TEASPOON VANILLA EXTRACT

¼ TEASPOON SALT

¼ TEASPOON GROUND NUTMEG

Heat the oven to 350 degrees F. Line a 9-inch pie pan with crust and then crimp the edges decoratively (see page 138). Line and partially bake the crust (see page 139). Increase the oven temperature to 425 degrees F.

In a medium saucepan, heat the milk over medium heat until it steams; look for tiny bubbles forming on the edge of the pan, and steam rising from the milk. Remove from the heat before it comes to a boil. Set aside. In a medium bowl, beat the eggs well. Stir in the sugar, vanilla, and salt, and stir well to dissolve the sugar and combine everything well.

Slowly pour in the milk, stirring with a whisk or a big wooden spoon. Pour the custard filling into the partially baked piecrust and sprinkle the nutmeg over the surface of the pie.

Place the pie on the bottom rack of the oven. Bake until the custard filling is mostly firm but still wiggly in the center, 25 to 35 minutes. Place the pie on a cooling rack or a folded kitchen towel and let cool to room temperature.

Buttermilk Pie

MAKES ONE 9-INCH PIE

Southerners have long loved baking with buttermilk, both for its tangy flavor and because it was a kitchen staple that needed to be used up. The pungently flavored, thick liquid remaining after you churned butter was considered a great treat by my grandfather and many other Southerners back in the day. But since most family members drank "sweet milk," as the non-buttermilk form was called, buttermilk went into biscuits, cornbread, and many a cake and pie, making them tender and rich. This homespun recipe makes buttermilk the starring ingredient in a marvelous and pleasing old-time pie. This pie will remind you of custard pie, but elevated to a complex deliciousness that you may, like me, come to crave. If you don't have buttermilk, look for buttermilk powder in the baking section of your grocery store, or add 1 tablespoon of lemon juice or vinegar to 1 cup of milk and let it stand for 10 minutes. It will develop a bit of body and sharpened flavor that will do the job.

PASTRY FOR A 9-INCH SINGLE-CRUST PIE (STORE-BOUGHT OR SEE BASIC PIECRUSTS, PAGE 134)

⅔ CUP SUGAR

3 TABLESPOONS FLOUR

1 CUP BUTTERMILK

¼ CUP BUTTER, MELTED

2 EGGS, BEATEN WELL

½ TEASPOON VANILLA EXTRACT

Heat the oven to 425 degrees F. Line a 9-inch pie pan with crust and then crimp the edges decoratively (see page 138).

In a medium bowl, combine the sugar and flour and use a fork to stir them together well. In another bowl, combine the buttermilk, butter, eggs, and vanilla, and use a whisk or a fork to mix them together very well. Add to the sugar-flour mixture and mix them together evenly and well.

Carefully pour the mixture into the pie shell and place it in the center of the oven. Bake for 10 minutes, then lower the heat to 350 degrees F. Bake until the edges puff up and the center is fairly firm, wiggling only a little when you gently nudge the pan, 20 to 30 minutes more. Place the pie on a cooling rack or a folded kitchen towel and let cool to room temperature.

Sweet Potato Pie

MAKES ONE 9-INCH PIE

This classic custard pie is perfectly wonderful in every way. You will find it on the dessert table in elegant Southern dining rooms and on makeshift tables at family reunions and church homecomings that feature dinner on the grounds. Sweet potatoes could be the most popular Southern pie filling of all if apples are taken out of the running. You'll find them as the filling for fried pies and small tartlets, often sold by the cash registers in old-school gas stations and twenty-first-century "convenience centers" alike, along the Southern backroads and interstates. Sweet potato pie holds pride of place in the African-American culinary repertoire, and versions abound—some a little sweeter, some velvety smooth, some generously spiced, and some not. Some boast the rustic texture of sweet potatoes cooked up in their jackets and mashed up by hand just before they're stirred into the pie. I adore this pie and I think it carries the profound messages of home and love in a particularly powerful and satisfying way. Should you have any remaining to be put away after supper, enjoy it come morning as an especially lovely breakfast food.

PASTRY FOR A 9-INCH SINGLE-CRUST PIE (STORE-BOUGHT OR SEE BASIC PIECRUSTS, PAGE 134)

I CUP SUGAR

½ TEASPOON GROUND CINNAMON

¼ TEASPOON GROUND NUTMEG

¼ TEASPOON SALT

1¼ CUPS EVAPORATED MILK OR HALF-AND-HALF

2 EGGS, BEATEN WELL

1½ CUPS MASHED, COOKED SWEET POTATOES (ABOUT 1½ POUNDS; SEE NOTE)

3 TABLESPOONS BUTTER, MELTED

I TEASPOON VANILLA EXTRACT

Heat the oven to 375 degrees F. Line a 9-inch pie pan with crust and then crimp the edges decoratively (see page 138).

Combine the sugar, cinnamon, nutmeg, and salt in a large bowl. Use a fork or a whisk to stir them together well. Add the milk and eggs, and stir to mix everything together evenly. Add the sweet potatoes, butter, and vanilla. Mix them together well, stirring them into the egg mixture carefully, until you have a thick, smooth, and evenly combined pie filling.

Pour the filling into the piecrust and place it on the middle rack of the oven. Bake until the edges puff up and the center is fairly firm, wiggling only a little when you gently nudge the pan, 50 to 55 minutes.

Place the pie on a cooling rack or on a folded kitchen towel and let cool for 30 minutes. Serve warm or at room temperature.

NOTE: To cook sweet potatoes for this pie, place 1½ pounds of whole, unpeeled sweet potatoes in a large pot with water to cover by 2 inches. Bring to a rolling boil over high heat. Reduce the heat to maintain a gentle boil and cook until the sweet potatoes are very tender. Depending on the size and shape, this will take between 15 and 30 minutes. Drain the sweet potatoes, and set them out on a platter until cool enough to handle. Peel the sweet potatoes, mash them well, and measure out 1½ cups.

Sweet Potato Pie

MAKES ONE 9-INCH PIE

Now the nationally renowned chef of Crook's Corner in Chapel Hill, North Carolina, Bill Smith is partial to the sweet potato pies stirred up by his father in New Bern, North Carolina. He uses sweetened condensed milk instead of evaporated or regular milk, giving his pies a smooth, rich texture, and seasons them boldly and wonderfully with allspice and cloves and a splash of lemon extract. Bill uses a stand mixer, which gives this pie a satiny texture and makes preparing it quick and simple. You can also use a handheld electric mixer or a whisk, eggbeater, or big wooden spoon. Whatever you use, you will be proud of your marvelous sweet potato pie.

PASTRY FOR A 9-INCH SINGLE-CRUST PIE (STORE-BOUGHT OR SEE BASIC PIECRUSTS, PAGE 134)

2 TABLESPOONS FLOUR

I TEASPOON GROUND CINNAMON

½ TEASPOON GROUND ALLSPICE

¼ TEASPOON GROUND CLOVES

¼ TEASPOON BAKING POWDER

¼ TEASPOON SALT

2 CUPS MASHED, COOKED SWEET POTATOES (ABOUT 2 POUNDS; SEE NOTE, PAGE 35)

2 EGGS

¾ CUP SUGAR

I CUP SWEETENED CONDENSED MILK

2 TABLESPOONS BUTTER, MELTED

¼ TEASPOON LEMON EXTRACT OR VANILLA EXTRACT

Heat the oven to 350 degrees F. Line a 9-inch pie pan with crust and then crimp the edges decoratively (see page 138).

In a small bowl, combine the flour, cinnamon, allspice, cloves, baking powder, and salt and use a fork to stir them together well.

Place the sweet potatoes in a medium bowl and beat them well, using an electric mixer at medium speed or a whisk or big wooden spoon. Add the eggs, one at a time, beating well after each addition.

Add the sugar and beat to incorporate it completely into the sweet potato–egg mixture. Add the spice mixture, milk, butter, and extract, and beat at low speed to combine everything evenly and well.

Pour the filling into the piecrust and place it on the lowest rack of the oven. Bake until the edges puff up and the center is fairly firm, wiggling only a little when you gently nudge the pan, 40 to 50 minutes.

Place the pie on a cooling rack or a folded kitchen towel and let cool to room temperature.

Irish Potato Pie

MAKES ONE 9-INCH PIE

Sweet potato is one of the best-loved pies in the Southern sweets pantheon, but fewer people remember the variation known as Irish potato pie. Also called white potato pie and simply potato pie, it's pure plain goodness, satisfying and flavored with cinnamon and nutmeg, as well as a splash of citrus. Enhancements abound for jazzing up this pie, from lemon extract, zest, or juice to fresh orange juice and zest, sweet spices, and a cloud of stiffly beaten egg whites folded into the custard before baking. The results are quite tasty, making for a hearty, homespun dessert from another time.

PASTRY FOR A 9-INCH SINGLE-CRUST PIE (STORE-BOUGHT OR SEE BASIC PIECRUSTS, PAGE 134)

¾ CUP SUGAR

½ TEASPOON BAKING POWDER

½ TEASPOON GROUND CINNAMON

¼ TEASPOON GROUND NUTMEG

¼ TEASPOON SALT

I CUP MILK

3 EGGS, BEATEN WELL

½ TEASPOON LEMON EXTRACT

2½ CUPS MASHED PEELED POTATOES (ABOUT 1½ POUNDS)

½ CUP BUTTER, MELTED

Heat the oven to 350 degrees F. Line a 9-inch pie pan with crust and then crimp the edges decoratively (see page 138).

In a small bowl, combine the sugar, baking powder, cinnamon, nutmeg, and salt, and use a fork to stir everything together well.

In a medium bowl, combine the milk, eggs, and extract, and stir to mix them well. Add the sugar mixture and stir to dissolve the sugar. Add the mashed potatoes and butter, and stir to mix everything together evenly and well. The mixture will be thick.

Transfer the filling to the piecrust. Place the pie on the bottom shelf of the oven. Bake until the filling is puffed up, nicely browned, and fairly firm, 40 to 50 minutes.

Place the pie on a cooling rack or a folded kitchen towel and let cool to room temperature.

Bean Pie

MAKES ONE 9-INCH PIE

Ever since I first tasted bean pie at The Know bookstore in Durham, North Carolina, I've been a fan. Given my deep affection for egg custard, pumpkin, and sweet potato pies, it's no surprise that I would adore bean pie, which shares culinary roots with those pie favorites. Developed in the 1930s as part of the nutritional teachings of the Nation of Islam, bean pies became standard items at black Muslim bakeries in urban communities from Chicago and Oakland, California, to Detroit and Washington, D.C. Navy beans are most commonly cited in recipes, but great Northern beans and pinto beans are also popular choices. With a can of beans and the usual custard pie ingredients, you can turn out a delicious bean pie fast. You can use a blender or a food processor to mix up your filling, or mash the cooked, drained beans well with a potato masher or a fork.

PASTRY FOR A 9-INCH SINGLE-CRUST PIE (STORE-BOUGHT OR SEE BASIC PIECRUSTS, PAGE 134)

1 CUP SUGAR

1 TABLESPOON FLOUR

½ TEASPOON GROUND CINNAMON

½ TEASPOON GROUND NUTMEG

½ CUP EVAPORATED MILK OR HALF-AND-HALF

¼ CUP BUTTER, MELTED

2 EGGS

1 TABLESPOON VANILLA EXTRACT

1 CUP MASHED, COOKED NAVY BEANS

Heat the oven to 350 degrees F. Line a 9-inch pie pan with crust and then crimp the edges decoratively (see page 138).

In a medium bowl, combine the sugar, flour, cinnamon, and nutmeg, and stir with a fork to mix well. Add the milk, butter, eggs, and vanilla, and stir to mix everything well. Add the mashed beans and use an electric mixer or a whisk to beat all the ingredients together well, making a thick, smooth filling.

Pour the filling into the piecrust. Place the pie on the bottom shelf of the oven. Bake until the edges puff up and the center is fairly firm, wiggling only a little when you gently nudge the pan, 40 to 50 minutes.

Place the pie on a cooling rack or a folded kitchen towel and let cool for 20 to 30 minutes. Serve warm or at room temperature.

A CHESS PIE COMPENDIUM

Along with custard pies, their close cousins, chess pies comprise the broadest category of traditional Southern pies. These are simple, rich pies, built on a luscious combination of eggs, butter, and something truly sweet, such as molasses, sorghum syrup, or brown or white sugar. Beyond these three common ingredients and a texture that is satiny smooth, variations abound. Some chess pies include cornmeal or flour, and some include a generous splash of vinegar or lemon juice. Transparent Pie (page 45) is a chess pie enriched with cream or milk, and Syrup Pie (page 46) depends on pure cane syrup, sorghum, or molasses for its signature sweetness. Not only do the ingredients vary, the intriguing name remains a mystery.

Nobody knows exactly where the word "chess" came from in relation to this beloved category of Southern pies, though mispronunciation is the constant among speculative stories. Some say it's from "chest," because the pie would have been stored in a pie safe, a wooden cupboard with deep shelves and doors of perforated tin and later screen, so that the pies could cool easily while keeping flies and pie-fans away until serving time. Since these cupboards have long been known as "pie safes" and have served to store countless flavors of pie, this idea doesn't work.

Others say that the name came from a modest Southern cook who answered a query as to the pie's name with a bashful, "It's just pie…." Like the cupboard story, this one makes little sense.

My money is on the British sweets kitchen, where "cheese pies" were made with sugar, butter, and eggs, but without any cheese. Early British cheese pies and cheese cakes meant ones with curds or curdled fillings, and "cheese" referred to "curds" and curdling, the thickening up of the ingredients into a firm filling. This theory can't be proven either, but the crucial points are quite clear: Chess pies have been enjoyed for a long time, and are quite simple to make at home. Given that history, they will no doubt remain on the A-list of Southern sweets for a long time to come.

(continued)

Southern cooks also know to put whatever nuts are handy into a sweet mixture and bake it up, giving the world Pecan Pie (page 55), Virginia peanut pie, black walnut pie, peanut butter cream pie (page 114), and hickory nut pie, as well as oatmeal pie—likely what cooks turned to when last autumn's nuts were all gone and the hankering for a pie with crunch and sweetness was too powerful to resist. Today's chefs are still inspired by the sweet-and-gooey pie theme epitomized by chess pies. Chef Barry Maiden, a southwestern Virginia native making waves with his Cambridge, Massachusetts, restaurant, built on his grandmother's pecan pie recipe to create his superb Hungry Mother Spicy Peanut Pie (page 56). Mississippi pastry chef and cookbook author Martha Hall Foose gladdened Southern hearts forever when she dreamed up Sweet Tea Pie (page 53) for a dessert competition a few years back. These inspired Southern pies move us forward without eclipsing the past.

Meanwhile, chess pie is alive and well and on the Southern table in multiple traditional forms. Here you'll find three standard chess pies, one with cornmeal and vinegar, one more in the straight-up-sweet mode, and Chef Leah Chase's divine version of Lemon Chess Pie (page 52). There's also Karen Wilcher's family favorite (page 51)—a chess pie spiked with just enough buttermilk for a fantastically tangy little edge. No wonder her great-aunt always had to make two; one to serve at the family reunion, and a second one for Karen's daddy to take home.

Molasses Pie

MAKES ONE 9-INCH PIE

This heirloom pie has gone out of favor, perhaps because molasses is no longer a standard kitchen ingredient as it was in the Southern kitchen until the 1960s. Pecan pie, the most popular variation on the chess pie theme, is usually made with corn syrup, and that milder flavor has captured our hearts and palates in the modern world. Molasses pie is a keeper though, so do try it. You'll find it's a lovely postcard from the Southern country kitchens and tables of more than one hundred years ago.

PASTRY FOR A 9-INCH SINGLE-CRUST PIE (STORE-BOUGHT OR SEE BASIC PIECRUSTS, PAGE 134)

½ CUP SUGAR

½ CUP ALL-PURPOSE FLOUR

½ TEASPOON GROUND CINNAMON

½ TEASPOON GROUND ALLSPICE OR NUTMEG

½ TEASPOON SALT

1 CUP SOUR MILK OR BUTTERMILK (SEE NOTE)

1 TEASPOON BAKING SODA

¾ CUP MOLASSES

3 EGGS, BEATEN WELL

2 TABLESPOONS BUTTER, MELTED

1 TABLESPOON FRESHLY SQUEEZED LEMON JUICE, OR WHITE OR APPLE CIDER VINEGAR

Heat the oven to 375 degrees F. Line a 9-inch pie pan with crust and then crimp the edges decoratively (see page 138).

In a medium bowl, combine the sugar, flour, cinnamon, allspice, and salt. Use a fork to stir these dry ingredients together well.

In a large bowl, combine the milk and baking soda and stir well. Whisk in the molasses. Add the eggs, butter, and lemon juice. Stir well, scraping the bowl and mixing everything into a thick, dark, rich filling.

Pour the filling into the piecrust. Place the pie on the bottom shelf of the oven. Bake for 10 minutes. Reduce the heat to 350 degrees F, and continue baking until the filling has puffed up and is handsomely brown and fairly firm, wiggling only a little when you gently nudge the pan, 35 to 40 minutes.

Place the pie on a cooling rack or a folded kitchen towel and let cool to room temperature.

NOTE: If you don't have sour milk or buttermilk handy, combine 1 cup of milk with 1 tablespoon of vinegar or lemon juice. Stir well and let stand 10 to 15 minutes, until milk thickens up and develops a tangy flavor.

Brown Sugar Pie

MAKES ONE 9-INCH PIE

Simple, sweet, rich goodness here. This pie calls for butter creamed with brown sugar, almost like the first stage of mixing up a butter cake. A little stirring and you'll have a grand treat. Look for organic or fair-trade brown sugar, which is typically made in a more traditional way and brings an intense, robust flavor to this old-school pie. It's available in specialty supermarkets, and by mail order (see page 156).

PASTRY FOR A 9-INCH SINGLE-CRUST PIE (STORE-BOUGHT OR SEE BASIC PIECRUSTS, PAGE 134)

½ CUP BUTTER, SOFTENED

2 CUPS PACKED DARK OR LIGHT BROWN SUGAR

3 EGGS

1 TEASPOON VANILLA EXTRACT

Heat the oven to 450 degrees F. Line a 9-inch pie pan with crust and then crimp the edges decoratively (see page 138).

In a medium bowl, beat the butter with a whisk or a big wooden spoon, until it is soft and creamy. Add the sugar and beat well, to combine the ingredients evenly and smoothly. Add the eggs, one by one, stirring well each time. Add the vanilla, stir to mix everything once more, and pour it into the piecrust.

Place the pie on the bottom shelf of the oven. Bake for 5 minutes. Reduce the heat to 350 degrees F and bake until the edges puff up and the center is fairly firm, wiggling only a little when you gently nudge the pan, 25 to 35 minutes more.

Place the pie on a cooling rack or a folded kitchen towel and let cool to room temperature.

Transparent Pie

The call for transparency in government rings loudly today; perhaps it would be heeded with more vigor were we to accompany it with generous slices of transparent pie. An old-time recipe with strong roots in Kentucky and Tennessee, transparent pie is chess pie with a twist—a generous splash of cream or milk in addition to the standard chess pie ingredients of eggs, butter, sugar, and flour. The big question, which I plan to research with tenacity and vigor: Is it true that Kentucky native and actor George Clooney totes transparent pies from Maysville, Kentucky, to the movie set to share with his colleagues? Stay tuned, and I'll get back to you on that. Meanwhile, feast on the sweet pleasure of this transparent pie, and consider a trip to Maysville come October, for its Transparent Pie and Folklife Festival.

PASTRY FOR A 9-INCH SINGLE-CRUST PIE (STORE-BOUGHT OR SEE BASIC PIECRUSTS, PAGE 134)

2 CUPS SUGAR

2 TABLESPOONS FLOUR

¼ TEASPOON SALT

¾ CUP EVAPORATED MILK

½ CUP BUTTER, MELTED

4 EGGS, BEATEN WELL

I TEASPOON VANILLA EXTRACT

Heat the oven to 375 degrees F. Line a 9-inch pie pan with crust and then crimp the edges decoratively (see page 138).

In a medium bowl, combine the sugar, flour, and salt. Stir with a fork or whisk to mix them together well. Add the milk, butter, eggs, and vanilla and beat well to combine everything into a smooth filling. Pour into the piecrust.

Place the pie on the bottom shelf of the oven. Bake until the edges puff up and the center is fairly firm, wiggling only a little when you gently nudge the pan, about 45 minutes.

Place the pie on a cooling rack or a folded kitchen towel and let cool to room temperature.

Syrup Pie

MAKES ONE 9-INCH PIE

This is good and plain and pure, just like the syrup in the pitcher on the kitchen table in many an old-time Southern home. You could use sorghum syrup, which is still being made throughout the southern Appalachian mountains by small, artisan producers. You could also use Steen's Pure Cane Syrup, which is still produced in the open-kettle, nothing-added, nothing-extracted, old-school way down at the C.S. Steen Syrup Mill in Abbeville, Louisiana. Both are culinary treasures, and the best way to keep the traditions around these two products is to find them, buy them, and use them. It will be your pleasure to do so, and a privilege, not a chore.

Regional recipes may refer to either one of these distinctive syrups as "molasses," since the term once served to mean "the sweet, dark, rich, and indispensable syrup we use and love around here." You could use either one in this pie, and you could also use molasses made from sugarcane or sugar beets, or even maple syrup—which is, as I understand it, "the sweet, dark, rich, and indispensable syrup they use and love a good ways north of here." Whipped cream or vanilla ice cream is a great companion to this pie, to my mind.

PASTRY FOR A 9-INCH SINGLE-CRUST PIE (STORE-BOUGHT OR SEE BASIC PIECRUSTS, PAGE 134)

2 CUPS SORGHUM, PURE CANE SYRUP, MOLASSES, OR MAPLE SYRUP

⅓ CUP EVAPORATED MILK OR HALF-AND-HALF

3 EGGS, BEATEN WELL

2 TABLESPOONS ALL-PURPOSE FLOUR

1 TEASPOON VANILLA EXTRACT

Heat the oven to 350 degrees F. Line a 9-inch pie pan with crust and then crimp the edges decoratively (see page 138).

In a medium bowl, use a fork or a whisk to beat the syrup, milk, eggs, flour, and vanilla, and stir to mix everything evenly and well. Pour into the piecrust.

Place the pie on the bottom shelf of the oven. Bake until the edges puff up, and the center is fairly firm, wiggling only a little when you gently nudge the pan, 40 to 45 minutes. A knife inserted into the filling about 1 inch from the edge of the pie should come out clean when the pie is done. Place the pie on a cooling rack or a folded kitchen towel and let cool. Serve warm or at room temperature.

Vinegar Pie

MAKES ONE 9-INCH PIE

Popular since colonial days and with a wide range of opinions on how intensely the startling main ingredient should figure in its namesake pie, it's small wonder that vinegar pie shows up all around the country. Southerners may not own it, but they sure do love it, as evidenced by its abundance in historic kitchen literature. Seldom seen outside of home kitchens, vinegar pie is a simple pleasure, slightly tart without being sour. Apple cider vinegar is my favorite, but most any vinegar would do except for balsamic, which is a bit too sweet and rich for vinegar pie. People often add a little splash of lemon extract, which is lovely, but I love the acidic edge of vinegar on its own.

PASTRY FOR A 9-INCH SINGLE-CRUST PIE (STORE-BOUGHT OR SEE BASIC PIECRUSTS, PAGE 134)

1½ CUPS SUGAR

1 TABLESPOON FLOUR

¼ TEASPOON SALT

3 EGGS, BEATEN WELL

¼ CUP BUTTER, MELTED

3 TABLESPOONS EVAPORATED MILK, HALF-AND-HALF, OR MILK

¼ CUP APPLE CIDER VINEGAR OR WHITE VINEGAR

Heat the oven to 350 degrees F. Line a 9-inch pie pan with crust and then crimp the edges decoratively (see page 138).

In a small bowl, combine the sugar, flour, and salt. Use a fork to stir them together well.

In a medium bowl, use a fork or a whisk to beat together the eggs, butter, and milk, and stir to mix everything together well. Add the sugar-flour mixture and stir it in well. Add the vinegar and mix to combine everything into a thick, smooth filling. Pour the filling into the piecrust.

Place the pie on the bottom rack of the oven. Bake for 10 minutes, and then reduce the heat to 325 degrees F. Bake until the edges puff up and the center is fairly firm, wiggling only a little when you gently nudge the pan, 35 to 45 minutes more.

Place the pie on a cooling rack or a folded kitchen towel and let cool to room temperature.

Old-Time Chess Pie

MAKES ONE 9-INCH PIE

This simple combination of eggs, butter, sugar, flour, and vanilla makes a delectable old-school chess pie. Luscious and sweet, it is one of the quickest pies in the Southern baking repertoire, and also one of the most cherished, past and present. If you're looking for a pie that travels well and wins major praise for minimal effort, this one will suit your purposes well.

PASTRY FOR A 9-INCH SINGLE-CRUST PIE (STORE-BOUGHT OR SEE BASIC PIECRUSTS, PAGE 134)

2 CUPS SUGAR

2 TABLESPOONS FLOUR

½ CUP BUTTER, MELTED

4 EGGS, BEATEN WELL

½ TEASPOON VANILLA EXTRACT

Heat the oven to 400 degrees F. Line a 9-inch pie pan with crust and then crimp the edges decoratively (see page 138).

In a large bowl, combine the sugar and flour, and stir with a fork to mix them well. Add the butter, eggs, and vanilla. Using a fork or a whisk, stir well to combine everything into a smooth, thick filling. Pour the filling into the piecrust.

Place the pie on the bottom shelf of the oven. Bake for 10 minutes. Lower the heat to 350 degrees F, and bake until the edges puff up and the center is fairly firm, wiggling only a little when you gently nudge the pan, 30 to 40 minutes more.

Place the pie on a cooling rack or a folded kitchen towel and let cool to room temperature.

Classic Chess Pie

MAKES ONE 9-INCH PIE

My friend Caryl Price told me her mom, Betty Thomason, makes a fabulous chess pie, and she was right. With her recipe, you can make this traditional treasure a standard part of your dessert repertoire. She includes a spoonful of cornmeal and a splash of vinegar, two unlikely ingredients that are often used in the filling for chess pies. Growing up on this pie may be the secret of Caryl's magnificently beautiful singing voice.

PASTRY FOR A 9-INCH SINGLE-CRUST PIE (STORE-BOUGHT OR SEE BASIC PIECRUSTS, PAGE 134)

1½ CUPS SUGAR

I TABLESPOON CORNMEAL

¼ TEASPOON SALT

3 EGGS, BEATEN WELL

I TABLESPOON APPLE CIDER VINEGAR OR WHITE VINEGAR

I TEASPOON VANILLA EXTRACT

½ CUP BUTTER, MELTED

Heat the oven to 325 degrees F. Line a 9-inch pie pan with crust and then crimp the edges decoratively (see page 138).

In a medium bowl, combine the sugar, cornmeal, and salt, and stir together well. Add the eggs, vinegar, and vanilla and use a fork or a whisk to stir them together well. Add the butter and stir well to combine everything into a smooth, thick filling. Pour it into the piecrust.

Place the pie on the bottom shelf of the oven. Bake until the edges puff up and the center is fairly firm, wiggling only a little when you gently nudge the pan, 40 to 45 minutes.

Place the pie on a cooling rack or a folded kitchen towel and let cool to room temperature.

Buttermilk Chess Pie

MAKES TWO 9-INCH PIES

My friend Karen Wilcher shared this lovely recipe, which makes two beautiful pies. Karen's great-aunt always made a pair of buttermilk chess pies for her family reunions in Kentucky. She put one out on the massive dessert table, and sent the other one home with Karen's father, who loved them so much that he needed one to call his own. Buttermilk enhances the filling, adding a creamy texture and nearly irresistible tangy flavor note to the pies.

PASTRY FOR TWO 9-INCH SINGLE-CRUST PIES (STORE-BOUGHT OR SEE BASIC PIECRUSTS, PAGE 134)

2 CUPS SUGAR

2 TABLESPOONS ALL-PURPOSE FLOUR

⅔ CUP BUTTERMILK

5 EGGS, SLIGHTLY BEATEN

2 TEASPOONS VANILLA EXTRACT

½ CUP BUTTER, MELTED

Heat the oven to 350 degrees F. Line two 9-inch pie pans with crust and then crimp the edges decoratively (see page 138).

In a large bowl, combine the sugar and flour and use a fork to stir them together. Add the buttermilk, eggs, and vanilla, and stir well. Add the butter and stir to blend everything together into an even filling. Divide the filling between the two piecrusts.

Place the pies on the bottom shelf of the oven. Bake until the edges puff up and the centers are fairly firm, wiggling only a little when you gently nudge the pans, 40 to 45 minutes.

Place the pies on a cooling rack or a folded kitchen towel and let cool to room temperature.

Lemon Chess Pie

MAKES ONE 9-INCH PIE

When legendary New Orleans Chef Leah Chase won the "Women Who Inspire" Lifetime Achievement Award from Women Chefs and Restaurateurs, she was delighted but a bit surprised. Sure, she's renowned as a chef, businesswoman, author, teacher, patron of the arts, parent, and community leader. True, luminaries from the worlds of politics, government, arts, entertainment, and business have dined gratefully at her restaurant, Dooky Chase, for more than fifty years, and her name is known in culinary circles around the world. But what's the fuss, she wondered? She's simply out there doing what she has to do, working hard, creating things, speaking out, mentoring, and making the world a better place, in and out of the kitchen. When Hurricane Katrina flooded her beautiful dining rooms with six feet of water, she waited for the waters to recede, and then put on her baseball cap, rolled up the sleeves of her chef's jacket, and marched in the kitchen door to get her stoves fired up once again. While her shrimp Clemenceau, gumbo z'herbes and trout amandine demand culinary expertise, her lemon chess pie is simple, straightforward, sunny, and wonderful, just like Mrs. Chase herself.

PASTRY FOR A 9-INCH SINGLE-CRUST PIE (STORE-BOUGHT OR SEE BASIC PIECRUSTS, PAGE 134)

2 CUPS SUGAR

2 TABLESPOONS CORNMEAL

1 TABLESPOON ALL-PURPOSE FLOUR

¼ TEASPOON SALT

4 EGGS, BEATEN WELL

¼ CUP BUTTER, MELTED

¼ CUP FRESHLY SQUEEZED LEMON JUICE

¼ CUP EVAPORATED MILK

2 TEASPOONS GRATED LEMON RIND OR ZEST

Heat the oven to 350 degrees F. Line a 9-inch pie pan with crust and then crimp the edges decoratively (see page 138).

In a medium bowl, combine the sugar, cornmeal, flour, and salt. Add the eggs, butter, lemon juice, milk, and lemon rind. Using a fork, mix well, stirring and scraping to combine everything evenly into a thick, smooth filling.

Pour into the piecrust and place the pie on the bottom shelf of the oven. Bake until the edges puff up and the center is fairly firm, wiggling only a little when you gently nudge the pan, 35 to 45 minutes.

Place the pie on a cooling rack or a folded kitchen towel and let cool to room temperature.

Sweet Tea Pie

Born and raised in the Mississippi Delta, Martha Hall Foose headed out to see the world and cooked her way through a mighty swath of it before moving back home to put down roots. Culinary school in France and working in professional kitchens from Austin and New Orleans to Minneapolis and Los Angeles taught her the foods of the world. In turn, she has taught the world about the culinary traditions of the South, through her restaurants, classes, and extraordinary first book, *Screen Doors and Sweet Tea: Recipes and Tales from a Southern Cook*. Martha dreamed up this recipe during her high school days, as her entry in the pie-baking contest at the Mississippi State Fair. She didn't win, but she should have; it's pleasure—pure and simple. For your ultimate Southern flavor, Ms. Foose suggests brewing an orange pekoe tea for this recipe, but she notes you can use the tea you like best. I'm fond of whipped cream with this pie, but it's just dandy even without it.

PASTRY FOR A 9-INCH SINGLE-CRUST PIE (STORE-BOUGHT OR SEE BASIC PIECRUSTS, PAGE 134)

2 CUPS SUGAR

1 CUP BUTTER, SOFTENED

8 EGG YOLKS

¾ CUP STRONG STEEPED TEA, AT ROOM TEMPERATURE

1 TABLESPOON FRESHLY SQUEEZED LEMON JUICE

1 TEASPOON GRATED LEMON ZEST

2 TABLESPOONS ALL-PURPOSE FLOUR

1½ TEASPOONS CORNMEAL

½ TEASPOON SALT

Heat the oven to 350 degrees F. Line a 9-inch pie pan with crust and then crimp the edges decoratively (see page 138).

In a large bowl, beat the sugar and butter on medium speed until light and fluffy. Add the egg yolks one by one, beating well each time. With the mixer off, add the tea, lemon juice, and lemon zest, and beat on medium speed to mix them in well. Add the flour, cornmeal, and salt, and use a fork or a whisk to stir them in evenly and well.

Pour the filling into the crust and place it on the bottom shelf of the oven. Bake until the edges puff up and the center is fairly firm, wiggling only a little when you gently nudge the pan, about 45 minutes.

Place the pie on a cooling rack or a folded kitchen towel and let cool to room temperature.

Pecan Pie

MAKES ONE 9-INCH PIE

Though this holds first place in many hearts when the subject of favorite Southern pies comes up, most people are surprised to learn that it is not particularly old, dating back only as far as the 1930s. I consider pecan pie a brilliant spin on the traditional Southern chess pie, which is the foundation for many of the greatest hits of Southern pies. This recipe for the classic favorite uses dark brown sugar instead of dark or light corn syrup, typical in many recipes. Molasses, sorghum, and pure cane syrup are also popular sweeteners for pecan pie. You could use either perfect pecan halves or chopped or broken pecan pieces. Both are excellent and traditional choices. I love the look of pecan halves, but for ease of cutting and serving, I usually chop them coarsely.

PASTRY FOR A 9-INCH SINGLE-CRUST PIE (STORE-BOUGHT OR SEE BASIC PIECRUSTS, PAGE 134)

I POUND DARK BROWN SUGAR (2 FIRMLY PACKED CUPS)

3 TABLESPOONS ALL-PURPOSE FLOUR

½ CUP BUTTER

I CUP MILK

3 EGGS

I TEASPOON VANILLA EXTRACT

1½ CUPS (ABOUT 6 OUNCES) PECANS, CHOPPED OR HALVES

Heat the oven to 350 degrees F. Line a 9-inch pie pan with crust and then crimp the edges decoratively (see page 138).

In a medium saucepan, combine the sugar and flour and stir to mix them together well. Add the butter and place the pan over medium heat. Cook, stirring and pressing the butter to melt it and combine it with the sugar. Remove the pan from the heat and set aside.

In a medium bowl, combine the milk, eggs, and vanilla. Stir well with a fork or a whisk to mix everything together evenly. While stirring gently, slowly pour the warm sugar mixture into the milk mixture. Mix to combine everything evenly and well. Pour the filling into the piecrust and sprinkle the nuts evenly over the top.

Place the pie on the bottom shelf of the oven. Bake until the edges puff up and the center is fairly firm, wiggling only a little when you gently nudge the pan, and it is nicely browned, 40 to 50 minutes. Place the pie on a cooling rack or a folded kitchen towel and let cool for at least 30 minutes. Serve warm or at room temperature.

Hungry Mother Spicy Peanut Pie

MAKES ONE 9-INCH PIE

Barry Maiden named his Cambridge, Massachusetts, restaurant Hungry Mother after a gorgeous state park near his hometown, in the blue-green mountains of southwestern Virginia. His Spicy Peanut Pie is a twenty-first-century chef's rendition of his grandmother's pecan pie, putting traditional ingredients—such as sorghum, peanuts, and bourbon—together with cayenne and chocolate chips, to make a fabulous pie. Sorghum can be found in some markets and ordered by mail (see page 156). If you can't find sorghum, you could use molasses, pure cane syrup, corn syrup, or even maple syrup. The spiced peanuts can be made a day in advance and stored in an airtight jar.

PASTRY FOR A 9-INCH SINGLE-CRUST PIE (STORE-BOUGHT OR SEE BASIC PIECRUSTS, PAGE 134)

SPICED PEANUTS
¼ CUP SUGAR

1½ TEASPOONS SALT

1 TEASPOON CAYENNE

1 CUP (4 OUNCES) UNSALTED ROASTED PEANUTS

FILLING
4 EGGS

1 CUP SORGHUM, MOLASSES, PURE CANE SYRUP, OR DARK CORN SYRUP

½ CUP PACKED DARK OR LIGHT BROWN SUGAR

3 TABLESPOONS BUTTER, MELTED AND COOLED SLIGHTLY

3 TABLESPOONS BOURBON (OPTIONAL)

2 TEASPOONS VANILLA EXTRACT

1 TABLESPOON ALL-PURPOSE FLOUR

1 CUP SEMISWEET CHOCOLATE CHIPS

Line a 9-inch pie pan with crust and then crimp the edges decoratively (see page 138). Line and fully bake the crust (see page 139). Let it cool to room temperature.

To make the spicy peanuts: Heat the oven to 350 degrees F. Line a baking sheet with parchment, waxed paper, or aluminum foil.

Make a simple syrup by combining the sugar and 2 tablespoons water in a small saucepan. Bring to a vigorous boil over medium-high heat, stirring to dissolve the sugar and create a smooth syrup. Remove from the heat and pour the syrup into a medium bowl. You should have about 2 tablespoons of clear thickened syrup.

Add the salt and cayenne to the syrup, and stir to mix them well. Add the peanuts to the syrup, and toss to coat them evenly and well. Spread the peanuts in a single layer on the prepared baking sheet.

Bake the peanuts until they are fairly dry and heated through, 5 to 10 minutes. Transfer them immediately to a large plate or platter to prevent sticking and to stop them from cooking further, and let them cool for about 20 minutes. When they are cool enough to handle, chop them coarsely and set aside.

To make the filling: In a medium bowl, stir the eggs together lightly, using a whisk or a fork. Add the sorghum and sugar and stir to combine everything into a smooth, thick mixture. Add the butter, bourbon (if using), and vanilla, and stir to mix everything together evenly and well. Stir in the flour, and then fold in the chopped peanuts.

Sprinkle ½ cup of the chocolate chips over the bottom of the piecrust and pour in the filling. Sprinkle the remaining chocolate chips on top of the pie. Put the pie on the middle shelf of the oven. Bake until the edges puff up and the center is fairly firm, wiggling only a little when you gently nudge the pan, 25 to 35 minutes.

Place the pie on a cooling rack or a folded kitchen towel and let cool to room temperature.

SPRING and SUMMER PIES

When springtime slips into the Southern landscape in the form of blooming red-bud and dogwood trees and choirs of crocus and daffodils, you can be sure that many a Southern cook heads straight for the shed, eager to move forward on this year's garden. Flowers are fine, but for cooks with green thumbs, it's time to check the backyard, to see if the pie plant is calling out to be made into that harbinger of spring, rhubarb pie. Legendary chef and cookbook author Bill Neal writes that he didn't know rhubarb by any other name than "pie plant" until he was grown. The English roots of the South show in this affection for rhubarb, as it has figured in English cookery for going on two hundred years. Paired with strawberries, which show up about a month later, rhubarb shows off in gorgeous lattice-topped pies (page 139).

Blueberries come next, with blackberries not far behind, just as it turns too hot to think and too hot to cook. What with air-conditioning, though, and the sheer passion for deep-dish blackberry cobbler (page 73), we do it anyway, and enjoy a cool piece in the porch swing, after sunset, chilled to the max with a big ol' scoop of vanilla ice cream. Peaches put themselves out there as summer really takes hold, giving you the opportunity to enjoy Nathalie Dupree's Peaches and Cream Pie (page 65), a stir-me-up sensation that seems like it must have taken time, but didn't. For a show-stopping summer confection, make Sandra Gutierrez's Peach-Pecan Pie (page 66). Crunchy cinnamon-kissed pecans make summer's best peaches even more delightful, and the pie tastes wonderful chilled or at room temperature.

For the season's most surprising pie, cook up Aunt Marian's Summer Squash Custard Pie (page 72). It's the best solution to the gardener's too-many-zucchini challenge, and it makes one fine breakfast as well as a summer supper finale. Saying good-bye to summer's pleasures is easier when you see the first scuppernong grapes of the year, round and juicy and calling all cooks to try Miss Letha's Scuppernong Meringue Pie (page 68). It feels like a farewell to summer, while the gardener's delight, Green Tomato Pie (page 71), gives comfort to cooks who might be sad to see their end-of-season tomatoes staying green on the vines. After a bite or two, any doubters will be won over to the quirky but delicious flavor of this practical treat.

Strawberry Icebox Pie

MAKES ONE 9-INCH PIE

This cool pink pie couldn't be much simpler, nor much more lovely on a hot summer evening when you hanker for something luscious. You cook up a quick strawberry jam, and stir it into whipped cream for a plush expansion on the glories of each—bright color and flavor from the berries; rich cool texture from the cream. Icebox pies often utilize gelatin or stiffly beaten egg whites for their firm texture; this pie calls on cornstarch and cream, like a substantially anchored version of the English treat known as a "fool." You can make this with blackberries or raspberries as well, and frozen berries will work nicely if you can't make it home from the farm stand without eating most of the berries you bought fresh.

ONE 9-INCH GRAHAM CRACKER CRUST (STORE-BOUGHT OR SEE PAGE 146)

⅓ CUP CORNSTARCH

6 CUPS HULLED, COARSELY CHOPPED STRAWBERRIES, FRESH OR FROZEN (ABOUT 1½ POUNDS)

I CUP SUGAR

⅛ TEASPOON SALT

2 TEASPOONS BUTTER

½ TEASPOON VANILLA EXTRACT OR ALMOND EXTRACT

1¼ CUPS HEAVY CREAM

2 CUPS FRESH STRAWBERRIES, SLICED (ABOUT 8 OUNCES; OPTIONAL)

Line a 9-inch pie pan with crust and then pinch edge to form a lip. Bake the crust as directed in the recipe.

In a small bowl, combine the cornstarch and ⅓ cup cold water. Stir with a spoon to combine them well, dissolving any lumps.

In a medium saucepan, combine the chopped strawberries, sugar, and salt. Stir to combine the fruit and sugar, and then cook over medium heat until the mixture comes to a gentle boil. Cook, stirring often, until the berries create a pool of sauce, about 5 minutes.

Stir up the cornstarch-water mixture, and add it to the pan. Cook, stirring often, until the strawberry sauce boils again, thickens up, and the berries are soft, 3 to 4 minutes more.

Remove from the heat, stir in the butter and vanilla, and set aside to cool to room temperature.

Beat the cream in a large bowl until it is very thick and luscious, holding its shape in round medium peaks that are not cottony-stiff. Stir in the strawberry jam mixture and gently fold the cream and jam together to make an even, rich mixture.

Pile the filling into the graham cracker crust and refrigerate for 3 to 4 hours, until very cold and fairly firm. Serve cold, and if you have sliced strawberries, spoon a small pile of them alongside each piece of pie. Refrigerate any remaining pie for up to 1 day.

BETH TARTAN'S

Old-School North Carolina Rhubarb Pie

MAKES ONE 9-INCH PIE

Rhubarb Pie was clearly dear to the heart of Elizabeth Hedgecock Sparks, who wrote under the name "Beth Tartan" as the beloved and highly respected food editor of the *Winston-Salem Journal* for many years. Her cookbook, ***North Carolina and Old Salem Cookery***, self-published in 1951, is a treasure—both for her witty and encouraging voice, and for the archive of culinary history preserved in its pages. She writes, "In making pie plant pies, mothers used to tell daughters, 'Put in as much sugar as you would for any fruit pie and then add that much again. Turn your back and throw in another handful.' Even if it too(k) all the sugar in the house, it would be worth it to see the pretty pink juice that trickles out of a freshly baked rhubarb pie."

Like last summer's blackberry jam on the winter pantry shelf, this cookbook is ready when we are, sweet, intensely flavored, and worthy of being shared. Here is her recipe for rhubarb pie, written for readers who knew how much rhubarb made "a good deep pile" and how long it would likely take until a pie's "pastry is browned."

PASTRY FOR A 9-INCH DOUBLE-CRUST PIE (STORE-BOUGHT OR SEE BASIC PIECRUSTS, PAGE 134)

I CUP SUGAR, PLUS MORE IF NEEDED

4 TABLESPOONS FLOUR

PINCH OF SALT

⅛ TEASPOON GROUND NUTMEG

I TEASPOON GRATED LEMON RIND

ABOUT 3½ CUPS CHOPPED RHUBARB, CUT INTO I-INCH LENGTHS, PLUS MORE IF NEEDED

4 TABLESPOONS UNSALTED BUTTER, CUT INTO PIECES AND CHILLED

Heat the oven to 450 degrees F. Line a 9-inch pie pan with crust, leaving a 1-inch overhang (see page 138). Refrigerate the top crust until needed.

In a small bowl, mix sugar, flour, salt, nutmeg, and lemon rind. Sprinkle one-third of this mixture on the bottom of the piecrust. Add enough 1-inch lengths of rhubarb "to make a good deep pile." Sprinkle with remaining sugar mixture and butter.

Top with "gashed crust or lattice work" (see page 139). Bake at 450 degrees F for 10 minutes. Reduce heat to 350 degrees F, and continue baking until pastry is browned and bubbling pink juices escape from the slits in the top crust, about 40 to 50 minutes.

Strawberry-Rhubarb Lattice Pie

MAKES ONE 9-INCH PIE

If you want visible and edible proof that winter is going-going-gone, this pie is your ticket. A Southern springtime classic, strawberry-rhubarb pie combines two distinctly different harbingers of spring—firm squared rhubarb pieces with round red-ripe summery berries—resulting in one glorious and gorgeous pie. It's simple to make, simply beautiful, and simply delicious. You can even use frozen rhubarb and frozen strawberries here, adding them straight from the freezer, without thawing. Ice cream isn't required, but with a pink, juicy pie like this, it's never wrong.

PASTRY FOR A 9-INCH DOUBLE-CRUST PIE (STORE-BOUGHT OR SEE BASIC PIECRUSTS, PAGE 134)

1¼ CUPS SUGAR

⅓ CUP ALL-PURPOSE FLOUR

¼ TEASPOON GROUND CINNAMON

¼ TEASPOON SALT

3 CUPS CHOPPED FRESH RHUBARB, CUT INTO ½-INCH CHUNKS (ABOUT 1 POUND)

2 CUPS HULLED AND CHOPPED FRESH STRAWBERRIES, CUT INTO 1-INCH CHUNKS (ABOUT 8 OUNCES)

1 TABLESPOON FRESHLY SQUEEZED LEMON JUICE

2 TABLESPOONS COLD BUTTER, CUT INTO ¼-INCH CHUNKS

Heat the oven to 425 degrees F. Line a 9-inch pie pan with crust, leaving a 1-inch overhang (see page 138). Refrigerate the top crust until needed.

In a large bowl, combine the sugar, flour, cinnamon, and salt and use a fork or a whisk to stir them together well. Add the rhubarb, strawberries, and lemon juice and mix very gently using a large spoon. Scrape the mixture into the piecrust, and distribute the butter bits evenly over the strawberry-rhubarb filling. Top the filling with a lattice crust (see page 139).

Place the pie on a baking sheet to catch spills, and place it on the bottom rack of the oven. Bake for 15 minutes, and then lower the temperature to 350 degrees F. Bake until the pink filling bubbles up and the pastry is golden brown, 45 to 50 minutes more.

Place the pie on a cooling rack or a folded kitchen towel and let it cool for at least 15 minutes. Serve it warm or at room temperature.

NATHALIE DUPREE'S

Peaches and Cream Pie

MAKES ONE 9-INCH PIE

Nathalie Dupree put Southern cooking on the national and international map with a series of PBS cooking programs that introduced culinary traditions and created new ones for millions of eager cooks and eaters. Beloved as a teacher, food writer, author, and mentor, Nathalie has made a career of attracting the spotlight and then pulling friends and colleagues in to share it with her. After years in Atlanta, she now makes her home in the Low Country of South Carolina, cooking and writing her next book in a beautiful Charleston row house filled with great food, heavenly aromas, and good friends. Being from the Peach State originally, Georgia-born Nathalie shared one of her peachy pies with me, one that couldn't be much easier and delivers so much pleasure you'll think you wore yourself out making it.

PASTRY FOR A 9-INCH SINGLE-CRUST PIE (STORE-BOUGHT OR SEE BASIC PIECRUSTS, PAGE 134)

¾ CUP SUGAR

½ CUP ALL-PURPOSE FLOUR

2 CUPS SLICED FRESH OR FROZEN PEACHES (4 MEDIUM PEACHES)

I CUP HEAVY CREAM

Heat the oven to 350 degrees F. Line a 9-inch pie pan with crust and then crimp the edges decoratively (see page 138).

Combine the sugar and flour in a medium bowl and stir with a fork or a whisk to mix them well. Add the peaches and toss to coat them evenly with the sugar mixture.

Scoop the peaches and juices into the piecrust and spread them out in an even layer. Pour the cream over the peaches, and then poke and move the peaches about so that the cream covers them evenly.

Place the pie on the bottom shelf of the oven. Bake until the peaches are tender and the cream has made a soft custard around them, 35 to 40 minutes.

Place the pie on a cooling rack or a folded kitchen towel and let cool to room temperature.

Peach-Pecan Pie

MAKES ONE 9-INCH PIE

Two simple steps and you will have before you a fantastic pie, created by my friend Sandra Gutierrez. Stir up a custard, crumble up a pecan topping, and stand by for applause and recipe requests. A master cooking teacher, Sandra came up with the pie when she ran out of heavy cream and had sour cream on hand. The resulting custard, like pastry cream with an enchanting tangy flavor, makes a luscious foil for ripe plums or nectarines as well. Sandra suggested I enjoy it with a dollop of cinnamon-spiked whipped cream and, as usual, she was right. Delicious!

PASTRY FOR A 9-INCH SINGLE-CRUST PIE (STORE-BOUGHT OR SEE BASIC PIECRUSTS, PAGE 134)

FILLING
3 CUPS PEELED, SLICED PEACHES, FRESH OR FROZEN (6 MEDIUM PEACHES; SEE NOTE)

I CUP SUGAR
⅔ CUP SOUR CREAM
3 EGG YOLKS
2 TABLESPOONS ALL-PURPOSE FLOUR

PECAN CRUMB TOPPING
½ CUP COLD BUTTER
½ CUP SUGAR
⅓ CUP ALL-PURPOSE FLOUR
½ TEASPOON GROUND CINNAMON
½ CUP (2 OUNCES) CHOPPED PECANS

Heat the oven to 350 degrees F. Line a 9-inch pie pan with crust and then crimp the edges decoratively (see page 138).

To make the filling: Scatter the peaches over the bottom of the piecrust.

In a medium bowl, combine the sugar, sour cream, egg yolks, and flour. Using a whisk or a fork, stir to mix everything into a thick, rich sauce. Pour this evenly over the peaches.

Place the pie on the center shelf of the oven. Bake until the custard is set and the crust is handsomely browned, about 30 minutes.

To make the topping: In the bowl of a food processor, combine the butter, sugar, flour, and cinnamon. Pulse the machine on and off, until the mixture resembles small peas. (Or use a pastry blender or your hands to mix and mash up the dry ingredients with the butter, making a crumbly mixture.) Stir in the chopped pecans, and set aside.

Remove the pie from the oven, and scatter the topping all over the pie. Return to the oven and bake until the pie is golden brown, 10 to 15 minutes more.

Place the pie on a cooling rack or a folded kitchen towel and let cool for at least 45 minutes. Serve warm, or refrigerate and serve cold.

NOTE: You can use frozen peaches here, without thawing. Cut them crosswise into large chunks, so that you can quickly get them into the pie filling.

Scuppernong Meringue Pie

MAKES ONE 9-INCH PIE

Native to North America, scuppernong grapes grow wild as well as tamed throughout the South. Their massive, undulating vines graciously fill in backyard grape arbors in early summer, providing shade from summer's heat. Their plush, extraordinary grapes are perfect for eating out of hand as well as for making jelly, juice, wine, and pie. Growing up by the White Oak River along the North Carolina coast near Swansboro, Mrs. Letha Henderson learned early on to plant, catch, and gather in whatever goodness nature provided, including scuppernong and Muscadine grapes. Onslow County soil was kind to farm families like hers, who planted corn, sugarcane, vegetables, and feed for dairy cows. Her lovely recipe comes from *Coastal Carolina Cooking* by Nancy Davis and Kathy Hart.

PASTRY FOR A 9-INCH SINGLE-CRUST PIE (STORE-BOUGHT OR SEE BASIC PIECRUSTS, PAGE 134)

FILLING
I QUART SCUPPERNONG OR MUSCADINE GRAPES (ABOUT 1¾ POUNDS)

I CUP SUGAR

I CUP HEAVY CREAM OR HALF-AND-HALF

3 EGG YOLKS

I TABLESPOON CORNSTARCH

MERINGUE
3 EGG WHITES

6 TABLESPOONS SUGAR

Heat the oven to 300 degrees F. Set out two medium saucepans for cooking both the scuppernong grape skins and pulp. Line a 9-inch pie pan with crust and then crimp the edges decoratively (see page 138). Refrigerate it until needed.

To make the filling: Wash the grapes and then squeeze them out of their skins into one of the saucepans. Place the grape skins in the other, and add 2 tablespoons of water to each pan. Cook both skins and pulp over medium heat, until each is tender and softened, about 15 minutes.

Mash the skins well. Press the pulp through a fine-mesh strainer and into the pan of mashed grape skins, leaving the seeds behind in the strainer.

Add the sugar, cream, egg yolks, and cornstarch to the pan of mashed grapes. Using a fork or a whisk, stir to combine everything evenly and well. Pour the filling into the piecrust.

Place the pie on the bottom shelf of the oven. Bake the pie until it is puffy and set, about 45 minutes. Remove the pie from the oven to a cooling rack or a folded kitchen towel, while you make the meringue. Increase the oven temperature to 350 degrees F.

To make the meringue: In a large bowl, beat the egg whites with an electric mixer on medium speed until foamy. Increase the speed to high, and beat until the egg whites begin to thicken to the texture of cream. Add the sugar 2 tablespoons at a time, beating well each time, until the meringue is thick, shiny, and able to hold curly, firm peaks.

Spread the meringue evenly over the cooked pie filling, sealing the edges to the crust completely and then piling the egg whites higher in the center of the pie. Use a spoon to form curly peaks all over the meringue. Bake until the meringue is handsomely browned, 10 to 15 minutes.

Place the pie on a cooling rack or a folded kitchen towel and let cool to room temperature.

Green Tomato Pie

MAKES ONE 9-INCH PIE

Hard, unripe green tomatoes may seem an unlikely ingredient for a sweet Southern pie, but once you've tasted this treat, you'll understand why it has so many fans. Popular as a pie ingredient around the country, green tomatoes have a particular following in the South. From mid-August through the first frost, gardens start slowing down, and the bounty of green tomatoes tempts cooks to fry them up as a vegetable, can them as a tangy component of mincemeat, and slice and bake them in pies like this one. Not only are they treated like apples in pies, they are sometimes paired with apples as a pie filling—the two textures complementing each other nicely. To prepare the tomatoes, cut out their cores, and then slice each one very thinly crosswise. You can use vinegar in place of the lemon juice, with apple cider vinegar as first choice. Any kind except balsamic will do the job of bringing up the tangy contrast between the tomatoes and the sweet seasonings in this pie. Vanilla ice cream makes a perfect partner for this late-summer-into-fall pie.

PASTRY FOR A 9-INCH DOUBLE-CRUST PIE (STORE-BOUGHT OR SEE BASIC PIECRUSTS, PAGE 134)

1½ CUPS SUGAR

2 TABLESPOONS ALL-PURPOSE FLOUR

½ TEASPOON GROUND CINNAMON

½ TEASPOON GROUND NUTMEG

¼ TEASPOON SALT

4 CUPS VERY THINLY SLICED GREEN TOMATOES (ABOUT 3½ POUNDS; SEE HEADNOTE)

2 TABLESPOONS COLD BUTTER, CUT INTO SMALL CHUNKS

2 TABLESPOONS FRESHLY SQUEEZED LEMON JUICE OR 1 TABLESPOON VINEGAR

Heat the oven to 425 degrees F. Line a 9-inch pie pan with half of the crust, leaving a ½-inch overhang (see page 138).

In a medium bowl, combine the sugar, flour, cinnamon, nutmeg, and salt. Use a fork or a whisk to stir everything together well. Add the thinly sliced green tomatoes and toss gently to season them evenly and well.

Transfer the seasoned tomatoes to the piecrust, and arrange them so that they are mounded up a little in the center. Scatter the small butter pieces over the top of the filling, and then sprinkle on the lemon juice.

Roll the remaining crust into a 10-inch circle. Place the top crust over the tomatoes, pressing it down gently to touch the top of the tomato filling. Trim away the extra pastry around the edges, and press the top and bottom edges together firmly. Fold up the bottom edges and crimp them, or press down on the edge with the back of a fork, sealing and decorating the pie. Cut about 8 slits around the top of the crust, so that steam can escape during baking.

Place the pie on the bottom rack of the oven. Bake for 10 minutes. Reduce the heat to 350 degrees F and bake until the pie is bubbling with sweet juices and a handsome golden brown, 40 to 50 minutes more.

Place the pie on a cooling rack or a folded kitchen towel and let cool for at least 30 minutes. Serve warm or at room temperature.

AUNT MARIAN'S

Summary Squash Custard Pie

MAKES ONE 9-INCH PIE

My friend and fellow food writer Angela Knipple cherishes memories of childhood visits to her Great-Uncle Curtis and Great-Aunt Marian's big farm. Perhaps her passion for food, cooking, and sustainable agriculture took root during her summer days in their enormous garden. She loved weeding and harvesting vegetables, and turning her fingers a fabulous shade of purple while picking purple-hull peas. Meals were major delights of homegrown, homecooked goodness, including this beautiful summer squash pie—deliciously creamy, sweet, and a little bit tart. You could use yellow squash instead of zucchini, or do a combination of the two.

PASTRY FOR A 9-INCH SINGLE-CRUST PIE (STORE-BOUGHT OR SEE BASIC PIECRUSTS, PAGE 134)

6 MEDIUM ZUCCHINI OR YELLOW SQUASH (ABOUT 1 ½ POUNDS)

¾ CUP SUGAR

1 TABLESPOON CORNSTARCH

¼ TEASPOON GROUND NUTMEG

¼ TEASPOON SALT

½ CUP HEAVY CREAM

3 EGGS, BEATEN WELL

¼ CUP BUTTER, MELTED

1 TEASPOON VANILLA EXTRACT

½ TEASPOON WHITE VINEGAR

Heat the oven to 400 degrees F. Line a 9-inch pie pan with crust and then crimp the edges decoratively (see page 138).

Trim the ends of the zucchini and cut each squash lengthwise into quarters, turning each into four long strips. Cut away the pointed edge of each strip, removing and discarding the seeds. Line up the strips and cut each one crosswise into ½-inch chunks. You should have about 6 cups of chopped zucchini.

In a medium saucepan with a tight-fitting lid, bring ¾ cup water to a rolling boil. Add the chopped zucchini, cover, and cook until the zucchini is tender and bright green, softened, but still holding its shape without turning to mush, 4 to 5 minutes. Remove from the heat and drain well.

In a small bowl, combine the sugar, cornstarch, nutmeg, and salt. Stir with a fork to mix everything well. In a medium bowl, combine the cream, eggs, butter, vanilla, and vinegar. Using a

whisk or a fork, stir to combine everything well. Add the sugar mixture and stir to dissolve the dry ingredients and mix everything together into a thick, smooth filling.

Transfer the zucchini back to the empty saucepan and mash it to make it as soft and smooth as possible. Drain off any extra liquid that the zucchini releases. Measure it out, so that you have about 2½ cups. Fold the mashed, drained zucchini into the filling and stir to mix everything together well.

Pour the filling into the piecrust. Place the pie on the middle shelf of the oven. Bake for 10 minutes. Reduce the heat to 325 degrees F, and bake until the filling is firm and nicely browned, and a knife inserted in the center of the pie comes out clean, 30 to 40 minutes.

Place the pie on a cooling rack or a folded kitchen towel. Let cool to room temperature. Serve at room temperature or slightly chilled.

Old-Time Blackberry Cobbler

MAKES ONE 8- OR 9-INCH COBBLER

My friend and fellow food writer Karen Wilcher comes from a family of great cooks, so it's no surprise that her blackberry cobbler turns heads and attracts spoons at any gathering. The centerpiece of her family reunions in Mobile, Alabama, its old-time goodness shines on any dessert table. She makes it in an 8-inch square baking pan, creating a deep-dish cobbler with maximum surface area for my favorite part, the blackberry-enrobed pastry crust. You could also use a deep-dish 9-inch pie pan with excellent results. Frozen blackberries work fine here, if you can't manage to pick more than you can eat before arriving back in the summertime kitchen. The handsome lattice top lets the bubbling blackberry goodness shine through. The instructions take up some space, but don't be put off by that—this is so easy that once you have done it, you'll be able to turn out cobblers like this without glancing back at a book, just like Grandma used to do.

PASTRY FOR A 9-INCH DOUBLE-CRUST PIE (STORE-BOUGHT OR SEE BASIC PIECRUSTS, PAGE 134)

I CUP SUGAR

2 TABLESPOONS ALL-PURPOSE FLOUR

2 TEASPOONS VANILLA EXTRACT

6 CUPS FRESH BLACKBERRIES (ABOUT 1½ POUNDS)

2 TABLESPOONS COLD BUTTER, CHOPPED INTO SMALL PIECES

Heat the oven to 450 degrees F.

Roll out about one third of the dough and trim it to make a 9-inch square. Place it on a baking sheet lined with parchment, waxed paper, or aluminum foil. Place on the center shelf and bake until the pastry square is dry, lightly browned, and developing small bubbles over the surface, about 10 minutes. Set aside to cool and leave the oven on.

Roll out another third of the dough into a 10- or 11-inch square, and gently fit it into an 8- or 9-inch square baking pan. Cut the dough into pieces as needed to patch together a bottom crust, shaping it to cover the surface of the baking pan. Trim the dough to leave ½ inch overhang. This way you will have plenty of crust to fold back down as you finish the pie. Press firmly wherever there are seams in the dough, so that the pan is sealed completely to hold in the delicious bubbling filling as it bakes.

Set aside all the scraps and pieces of pie dough for finishing up the top lattice crust.

Combine the sugar and flour in a small bowl. Stir the vanilla into ¼ cup cold water. Place these two mixtures by the pastry-lined pan, along with the blackberries and the baked pastry square.

Scatter half the blackberries into the pan; they won't cover it completely and that is fine. Sprinkle half the sugar mixture over the berries, then sprinkle half the water over the sugared berries, and scatter half the small chunks of butter over them as well.

Place the baked piecrust square on top of the berries, and repeat the process, scattering in the remaining berries, sugar, water, and butter.

(continued)

Roll out the remaining pastry and scraps into a 10-inch square. Cut 14 long strips about 1½ inches wide. Drape 7 of the pastry strips over the berries in 1 direction, so that you have an inch or so of overhang past the edge of the pan. Drape the remaining 7 pastry strips at right angles to the first batch, in a criss-cross design, making a big, edible, tic-tac-toe board. Dip your fingers in water, and then dampen the underside of each strip end. Press each one against the crust, sealing it firmly against the pastry-covered side of the pan.

To finish the crust, fold the top edges of the piecrust up, enclosing and covering the strips and just touching the berries. Press to seal them against the sides of the pan. To seal the crust, you can pinch the dough into a crimped pattern, or press it flat against the sides of the baking pan with the back of a fork, making a design with the tines.

Place the pie on a baking sheet to catch spills, and place it on the bottom rack of the oven. Bake for 10 minutes, and then reduce the heat to 350 degrees F. Bake until the filling is juicy and bubbling up through the pastry strips, and the crust is golden brown, 45 to 50 minutes more. Place the pie on a cooling rack or a folded kitchen towel and let cool for 20 minutes. Serve warm or at room temperature.

FALL and WINTER PIES

Throughout the South, autumn arrives in vivid ways, both visible and tangible: leaves going from green to orange, red, and brown; short sleeves forsaken for jackets and sweaters; and the quality and amount of light softening and fading as the temperature drops. For many Southerners back in the day, it meant an end to often-ferocious heat, of long hours tending to the vegetable garden or steaming up the kitchen while canning and preserving the garden's bounty. It meant farewell to evenings spent chasing lightning bugs, or sitting out on the porch because it just got too hot in the house. As leaves turned and darkness came earlier in the evening, autumn food began to make sense: A fire in the woodstove or the heat from an electric range attracted family members to the kitchen, eager for hearty food, served warm from the stove or the oven. Nature offered reasons aplenty to bake up autumnal pies, from dozens of apple varieties to sweet, thick-skinned Muscadine grapes, sticky-ripe wild persimmons, plump pumpkins, crisp pears, and bushels of windfall pecans.

Fall in the South heralded a high season for pies, celebrated herewith starting with the letter "A," as in "autumn" and "apple." Apples mattered greatly in the rural South well into the twentieth century, with particular trees grown for cider, for drying, for apple butter, for keeping, and for pies. Here you'll find four apple pies, from past and present, rooted in the Mississippi Delta, the Blue Ridge mountains, and the red Georgia clay. Choose a keepsake in Miz Bob's Double Apple Pie (page 81) or Mrs. Abby Fisher's Cream Apple Pie (page 82). Enjoy Apple-Pecan Crumble Pie (page 84) from David Guas of DamGoodSweet, and Fried Apple Pies (page 78) from Virginia Willis, author of *Bon Appetit, Y'all!*

Forage a source for the fixings for Muscadine Grape Hull Pie (page 89), a homespun, double-crust sensation. Persimmon Pie (page 94) and *Winchester Sun* Pumpkin Pie (page 93) capture the flame-orange colors and flavors of fall with extra spice, and Blue Grass Cranberry Pie (page 92) provides a worthy and easy-to-make option for your holiday dessert table. Dr. George Washington Carver's Sliced Sweet Potato Pie (page 86) takes some time, but each step is simple and the result is a handsome and delicious old-timey dessert. Each of these pies is well worth making wherever you are cooking, to welcome or imagine the arrival of fall, or to sweeten and warm up your wintertime cooking. Warm pie is synonymous with "cozy kitchen," so get out your mixing bowl and decide where in the fall-to-winter pie invitational you would like to begin.

Fried Apple Pies

MAKES 12 TO 14 INDIVIDUAL PIES

My friend and fellow food writer Virginia Willis grew up in Georgia in a family of fine Southern cooks. Once grown, she headed to culinary school in France, where she earned a diploma at La Varenne, and stayed on to work with its inspiring founder, Anne Willan. Virginia's book, *Bon Appetit, Y'all!*, beautifully expresses what Virginia learned from life and food in both of her culinary homeplaces, France and the American South. She often weaves the two traditions together wonderfully, but not here. These fried apple pies are 100 percent Georgia home cooking. And since she's shared her recipe, you can add them to your home kitchen repertoire, no matter where you're cooking. Plan ahead when making these, as you will need to soak the dried apples for at least four hours before making the filling.

FILLING

10 OUNCES DRIED APPLES

½ CUP SUGAR

ABOUT 2 CUPS CANOLA OIL, FOR FRYING

PIECRUST DOUGH

2 ½ CUPS SELF-RISING FLOUR (SEE NOTE), PLUS MORE FOR DUSTING

½ CUP SOLID VEGETABLE SHORTENING, CHILLED

⅔ CUP BUTTERMILK

CONFECTIONERS' SUGAR, FOR SERVING

To make the filling: Place the apples in a large bowl. Add 6 cups cold water. Cover and set aside at room temperature to rehydrate for at least 4 hours or overnight.

Put the soaked apples and any remaining liquid in a large saucepan. Add 2 more cups of water and the sugar, and bring to a boil over high heat. Reduce the heat to maintain a simmer, and cook until the apples thicken up and begin to break down, about 1 hour. Remove from the heat and use a potato masher or a fork to mash the apples into a soft, chunky filling. If preparing in advance, cover and refrigerate for up to 1 day.

When ready to fry the pies, heat the oil in a large, deep, heavy-duty skillet over medium heat. You will need about 2 inches of canola oil for frying the pies. The temperature should read 350 degrees F when measured with a deep-fat thermometer.

Meanwhile, to make the piecrust dough: Using a pastry blender or 2 knives, cut the shortening into the flour until it resembles coarse meal. Add the buttermilk and stir until a dough forms. Transfer the dough to a work surface lightly dusted with flour. Knead until smooth. Pull off a biscuit-sized piece of dough. On the lightly floured surface, roll out the dough into a 4-inch circle (about the size of a teacup saucer).

Place about 2 tablespoons of the apple mixture in the center of the circle. Fold the dough over to form a half moon. Press with your fingertips to seal the edges. Dip the tines of a fork in flour, then press the tines of the fork around the edges of the dough to seal completely.

Transfer one pie at a time to the heated oil and cook it until golden brown, turning gently, about 2 minutes per side. Repeat with the remaining dough and apples. Dust with confectioners' sugar. Serve hot, warm, or at room temperature.

NOTE: If you don't have self-rising flour, here's a formula for making it: For each cup of self-rising flour, stir together 1 cup all-purpose flour, 1 teaspoon baking powder, ½ teaspoon salt, and ¼ teaspoon baking soda. For this particular recipe, to make 2½ cups of self-rising flour, stir together 2½ cups all-purpose flour, 2½ teaspoons baking powder, 1¼ teaspoons salt, and ¾ teaspoon baking soda.

Double Apple Pie

MAKES ONE 9-INCH PIE

My friend Kathy Starr grew up in Hollandale, Mississippi, where she learned about life and Southern cooking from her grandmother, Mrs. Frances Fleming Hunter. Known as "Miz Bob" to her friends, neighbors, and customers at the Fair Deal Café, Mrs. Hunter cooked fabulous hearty meals using fresh, local produce. Fresh, local, and sustainable are newly planted in our culinary vocabulary today, and rightly so, but reading Starr's moving memoir and cookbook, *The Soul of Southern Cooking*, reminds us that such modern brilliance is old-school wisdom that we set aside for too long. Miz Bob cooked the fruit for her pies on the stove, seasoning it with cinnamon and nutmeg and enriching it with butter before sealing it into a pastry crust. She cooked in two stages, placing a middle layer of piecrust dough on top of a half-filled pie to bake, then covering it with more fruit and a top crust.

PASTRY FOR THREE 9-INCH SINGLE-CRUST PIES (STORE-BOUGHT OR SEE BASIC PIECRUSTS, PAGE 134)

2 ¼ POUNDS COOKING APPLES, SUCH AS GRANNY SMITH, JONATHAN, ROME BEAUTY, OR EMPIRE

1 ½ CUPS SUGAR

1 ½ TEASPOONS GROUND CINNAMON

I TEASPOON GROUND NUTMEG

⅓ CUP BUTTER

¼ CUP WATER

2 TABLESPOONS ALL-PURPOSE FLOUR

Heat the oven to 375 degrees F. Line a 9-inch deep-dish pie pan with crust, leaving a ½-inch overhang (see page 138).

Peel the apples, core them, and cut them into slices ½ inch thick. (You'll have about 5 cups.) In a large saucepan, combine the apples, sugar, cinnamon, and nutmeg, and toss to combine evenly and well. Add the butter and water, and bring to a gentle boil over medium-high heat. Reduce the heat to maintain a gentle simmer, and cook until the apples are tender, about 20 minutes. Stir in the flour and cook, 10 minutes more, stirring now and then.

Pour half of the apple mixture into the piecrust. Roll half of the remaining dough into a 9-inch circle and place it over the apple filling in the pan. Place the pie on the center rack of the oven. Bake until the pastry is golden brown and the apple filling is bubbling, about 20 minutes.

Pour the remaining apple mixture into the piecrust, covering the cooked pastry. Using the back of a spoon, dab a little water on the strip of piecrust covering the rim of the pie pan. Roll the remaining dough into a 10-inch circle and place it carefully over the apple filling. Trim away the extra pastry extending beyond the rim of the pie pan.

To seal the top crust, use the back of a fork to press the top and bottom crusts together, working your way around the rim by pressing the tines of the fork into the pastry edge. Use a sharp knife to cut about 8 slits in the top crust, spacing them evenly, so that steam can escape and the filling can bubble up as it cooks.

Return the pie to the oven and bake until the pastry is golden brown and the filling is fragrant, 20 to 25 minutes more.

Place the pie on a cooling rack or a folded kitchen towel and let cool for 15 minutes. Serve warm or at room temperature.

Cream Apple Pie

MAKES ONE 9-INCH PIE

If you're short on the courage to pursue your dreams, let the spirit of Mrs. Abby Fisher inspire you to get out there and find out what you can do. A nineteenth-century entrepreneur who turned her culinary talents and business sense into a highly successful food manufacturing business, she made history in San Francisco in 1881 by adding "author" to her extraordinary resume. Born into slavery in South Carolina, she worked her way to Mobile, Alabama, as a young woman, where she married and raised eleven children. She later journeyed from the deep South to a new life in California, where she earned financial success, awards, and fame for her food products, including pickles, sauces, chutneys, jellies, and preserves. Her book, *What Mrs. Fisher Knows about Old Southern Cooking: Soups, Pickles, Preserves, Etc.*, provides us with a collection of classic Southern dishes, from roast beef and crab croquettes to oyster gumbo, jelly cake, and this lovely apple pie. Her book, reissued in the 1990s by Applewood Books, is a must for your library on Southern cuisine. Here is her recipe for Cream Apple Pie as written in her book, followed by my version.

"The best of apples to be used. To two pounds of apples use a gill of water; put on fire to steam till the apples will mash perfectly fine and soft; sweeten to taste and let them cool. Season with powdered cinnamon, one half teaspoon full of the best. Have one crust of pastry only, and that at the bottom of plate; fill plate with the fruit, then bake quickly in a hot oven. Take one pint of fresh cream sweetened to taste; beat the whites of five eggs light, and add to the cream; flavor with vanilla. Beat the cream lightly before adding the eggs, then with a spoon spread over pies on sending to the table."

PASTRY FOR A 9-INCH SINGLE-CRUST PIE (STORE-BOUGHT OR SEE BASIC PIECRUSTS, PAGE 134)

FILLING
2 POUNDS TART COOKING APPLES, SUCH AS GRANNY SMITH

¾ CUP SUGAR

½ TEASPOON GROUND CINNAMON

¼ TEASPOON SALT

1 CUP HEAVY CREAM

3 EGG YOLKS

MERINGUE
3 EGG WHITES

6 TABLESPOONS SUGAR

Heat the oven to 350 degrees F. Line a 9-inch pie pan with crust and then crimp the edges decoratively (see page 138). Line and partially bake the crust (see page 139).

To make the filling: Peel the apples, and then quarter them lengthwise. Cut away the core portion of each apple, and then chop them into large chunks. Put the apples in a medium saucepan with ⅓ cup water and bring to a boil over high heat. Reduce the heat to medium and cook until the apples are tender, 10 to 15 minutes. Remove from the heat and mash them into a fairly smooth puree. Add the sugar, cinnamon, and salt, and stir to mix well.

In a small bowl, combine the cream and egg yolks. Use a fork or a whisk to stir them together and combine them until smooth. Add the egg yolk mixture to the apple filling and stir to combine everything evenly and well.

Pour the apple filling into the piecrust and place the pie on the bottom rack of the oven. Bake until the filling is puffed up, fairly dry, and lightly browned, 20 to 25 minutes. Remove the pie to a cooling rack while you prepare the meringue.

To make the meringue: In a large bowl, beat the egg whites with an electric mixer on medium speed until foamy. Increase the speed to high, and beat until the egg whites begin to thicken to the texture of cream. Add the sugar 2 tablespoons at a time, beating well each time, until the meringue is thick, shiny, and able to hold curly firm peaks. Spread the meringue evenly over the cooked pie filling, sealing the edges to the crust completely and then piling the egg whites higher in the center of the pie. Use a spoon to form curly peaks all over the meringue. Return the pie to the oven and bake until the meringue is handsomely golden browned, 10 to 15 minutes more.

Place the pie on a cooling rack or a folded kitchen towel and let cool to room temperature.

Apple-Pecan Crumble Pie

MAKES ONE 9-INCH PIE

David Guas is a pastry chef based in Washington, D.C., whose family roots connect him to Louisiana and Cuba. His spectacular apple pie puts Southern standbys to work in a marvelous way, tumbling toasted pecans and Steen's Pure Cane Syrup with lemon and nutmeg to elevate a simple apple pie to fantastic heights. He suggests sturdy cooking apples such as Jonagolds, Staymans, or Granny Smiths, and notes that you can make the crumble in advance and store it in an airtight container in the freezer for up to three months.

Steen's Pure Cane Syrup is a smoother-flavored cousin of molasses; it is processed from sugarcane in Abbeville, Louisiana, and is available in specialty markets and by mail order (see page 156). You can substitute sorghum (see page 154), molasses, Lyle's Golden Syrup, or dark corn syrup if you don't have a sunshine-yellow can of Steen's. Ice cream or whipped cream would be lovely company for this pie.

PASTRY FOR A 9-INCH SINGLE-CRUST PIE (STORE-BOUGHT OR SEE BASIC PIECRUSTS, PAGE 134)

SALTED PECAN CRUMBLE
⅔ CUP (ABOUT 4 OUNCES) COARSELY CHOPPED PECANS

⅔ CUP ALL-PURPOSE FLOUR

2 TABLESPOONS PACKED LIGHT BROWN SUGAR

2 TABLESPOONS GRANULATED SUGAR

I TEASPOON SALT

½ TEASPOON GROUND CINNAMON

5 TABLESPOONS COLD BUTTER, CUT INTO PIECES

FILLING
6 TO 8 APPLES, SUCH AS JONAGOLDS, STAYMANS, OR GOOD OLD GRANNY SMITHS (ABOUT 2½ POUNDS)

½ CUP SUGAR

3 TABLESPOONS STEEN'S PURE CANE SYRUP, SORGHUM, MOLASSES, OR DARK CORN SYRUP

2 TABLESPOONS CORNSTARCH

1½ TEASPOONS GROUND NUTMEG

½ TEASPOON LEMON ZEST

Heat the oven to 350 degrees F. Line a 9-inch pie pan with crust and then crimp the edges decoratively (see page 138). Refrigerate it until needed.

To make the salted pecan crumble: Scatter the pecans on a baking sheet or in a cake pan, and bake until they are aromatic and lightly browned, 5 to 10 minutes. Turn the pecans out onto a plate and spread them out to cool for about 15 minutes.

In a food processor, combine the flour, sugars, salt, cinnamon, and ⅓ cup of the cooled pecans. Process the ingredients briefly, just to grind the pecans, about 30 seconds. Add the butter and pulse the machine on and off, just until the mixture is coarse and crumbly. Transfer the mixture to a medium bowl and add the remaining ⅓ cup pecans. Using your hands, crumble and squeeze the mixture to form larger clumps. Refrigerate for about 30 minutes, or until you are ready to complete the pie. (If you don't have a food processor handy, simply chop half of the toasted pecans on a cutting board, stir them together with the remaining crumble ingredients, and finish by hand.)

To make the filling: Peel the apples, core them, and cut them into slices ½ inch thick. (You'll have about 4 cups.) In a large bowl, combine the sugar, cane syrup, cornstarch, and nutmeg and stir with a fork to mix everything well. Add the apples and lemon zest, and then toss to coat the apples evenly with the sweet spice mixture.

Pour the apple mixture into the piecrust. Distribute the apples into a fairly even layer, and then sprinkle the chilled crumble evenly over the top of the apple filling, gently pressing the crumble to set it into place.

Place the pie on a baking sheet to catch drips and place it on the center shelf of the oven. Bake until the filling is bubbling and the crumble is golden brown, about 1 hour.

Place the pie on a cooling rack or a folded kitchen towel and let cool for 10 minutes. Serve warm or at room temperature.

Sliced Sweet Potato Pie

MAKES ONE 9-INCH PIE

When Dr. George Washington Carver wrote his *Agricultural Bulletin #38* in 1936, his goal was to provide African American farmers with much more than just guidance for raising sweet potatoes as a cash crop and food source. Already in his seventies, and more than four decades into his work as a research chemist, botanist, educator, and author, he tirelessly presented practical, focused information on agriculture, nutrition, and business practices, so that his readers could choose crops that might bring them financial benefits as well as nutritional ones. His bulletins began with notes on agricultural varieties and how to plant them with success, then moved on to dozens of recipes, including several for sweet potato pies. This one is my favorite.

Plan to take your time here, as this isn't the fastest pie in the book. The rewards are well worth your time. Carver liked spices as much as I do, but if you don't have all these in your pantry, you can simply season your pie with cinnamon, or a combination of your choosing. You could prepare this in advance by cooking the sweet potatoes and slicing them in one session, and then assembling and baking the pie the next day.

PASTRY FOR A 9-INCH DOUBLE-CRUST PIE (STORE-BOUGHT OR SEE BASIC PIECRUSTS, PAGE 134)

4 MEDIUM SWEET POTATOES (ABOUT 3 POUNDS)

1¼ CUPS SUGAR

2 TABLESPOONS ALL-PURPOSE FLOUR

1 TEASPOON GROUND ALLSPICE

½ TEASPOON GROUND GINGER

½ TEASPOON GROUND NUTMEG

¼ TEASPOON GROUND CLOVES

2 TABLESPOONS CREAM, EVAPORATED MILK, OR HALF-AND-HALF

⅓ CUP MOLASSES, SORGHUM, PURE CANE SYRUP, OR HONEY

½ CUP HOT WATER, RESERVED FROM THE SWEET POTATOES' COOKING LIQUID

3 TABLESPOONS COLD BUTTER, CHOPPED INTO SMALL BITS

Line a 9-inch deep-dish pie pan with dough, draping it over the edge of the pie pan with a 1½-inch border of pastry extending beyond the rim. Refrigerate until needed.

Place the whole, unpeeled sweet potatoes in a large pot with water to cover by 2 inches. Bring to a rolling boil over high heat. Reduce the heat to maintain a gentle boil, and cook until the sweet potatoes are tender enough to be sliced, but not so tender that they fall apart. Depending on their size and shape, this should take between 15 and 30 minutes. Remove any smaller sweet potatoes as they reach the right texture and let larger ones cook until they reach the correct texture.

While the sweet potatoes are cooking, prepare the seasonings. In a small bowl, combine the sugar, flour, allspice, ginger, nutmeg, and cloves. Stir with a fork to mix them together well.

In a medium bowl or a heatproof measuring cup, combine the cream and molasses. When the sweet potatoes are cooked, measure out ½ cup of their cooking water. Add this to the molasses and cream and stir to mix these liquids well.

(continued)

Drain the sweet potatoes and set them out on a platter to cool enough to be handled. Peel and trim the sweet potatoes. Slice them *lengthwise* into slabs about ¼ inch thick (see Note). You will need about 4 cups; enough slices to generously fill the piecrust.

Heat the oven to 350 degrees F. Roll out the top crust to about 11 inches in diameter.

Have the spice mixture, molasses mixture, and butter all ready. Place two layers of sweet potato slices in the bottom of the piecrust. Sprinkle about one third of the spice mixture over this first layer. Add another two layers of sweet potato slices, another third of the spice mixture, and finish up with a final two layers of sweet potato slices, filling the piecrust almost to the very top. Add a few slices of sweet potatoes to the center, to build it up a little higher. Sprinkle all the remaining spices over this third layer.

Pour the molasses mixture evenly over the filling (you may have extra, just use what you need), and place the bits of cold butter around the top of the pie. Cover the pie with the top crust. Fold the edges of the bottom crust up and over the top crust and press to seal them together well. Using the tines of a fork, work your way around the piecrust, pressing to make a handsome parallel design on the crust as you seal it. Use a sharp knife to cut eight slits in the top of the pie, so that steam can escape and the filling can bubble up through the crust.

Place the pie on a baking sheet on the center rack of the oven. Bake until the crust is nicely brown, the filling is bubbling, and the sweet potatoes are tender all the way through, 45 to 55 minutes.

Place the pie on a cooling rack or a folded kitchen towel and let cool to room temperature.

NOTE: You'll slice the sweet potatoes lengthwise into "planks," not crosswise into rounds.

Muscadine Grape Hull Pie

Sweet heavenly days! This is a pie from the past that belongs in the present and future! Profoundly purple with the color from the thick, pungent hulls of Muscadine grapes, this pie's sweet flavor is memorable and pure. Muscadine grapes are an American original, native to the wild woods of the Atlantic seaboard and over the Appalachian mountains. Southerners have never been at a loss as to what to do with such natural bounty, eating them out of hand, cooking them down into jellies and syrups, fermenting their juices into wine, and capturing their glory in this old-timey pie. You can use deep reddish colored Muscadines, tawny golden-green scuppernongs, or even Concord grapes—a northern cousin that is available more widely as a commercial crop. You'll find scuppernongs and Muscadines in eastern and southern farmers' markets, farm stands, and some supermarkets for a short window in the early fall. Buy some, eat them up, and cook them down, to enjoy through the winter in the traditional way.

PASTRY FOR A 9-INCH DOUBLE-CRUST PIE (STORE-BOUGHT OR SEE BASIC PIECRUSTS, PAGE 134)

¾ CUP SUGAR

¼ CUP ALL-PURPOSE FLOUR

¼ TEASPOON SALT

5 CUPS MUSCADINE GRAPES (ABOUT 2 POUNDS), RINSED

I TABLESPOON FRESHLY SQUEEZED LEMON JUICE

3 TABLESPOONS COLD BUTTER, CUT INTO SMALL PIECES

Heat the oven to 400 degrees F. Line a 9-inch pie pan with crust, leaving a 1-inch overhang (see page 138). Refrigerate the remaining dough.

In a small bowl, combine the sugar, flour, and salt, and stir with a fork to mix well. Set out a medium bowl and a medium saucepan.

Squeeze the grapes over the saucepan, dropping the pulpy, seed-filled grapes into the pan and placing their thick, sturdy skins or hulls into the medium bowl. Add 3 tablespoons of water to the saucepan and place it over medium heat. Bring to a gentle boil and cook the grape pulp until softened and shiny, about

5 minutes. Transfer the cooked grape pulp to a strainer and place it over the bowl of grape hulls. Press the grapes through the strainer, pushing the softened pulp into the bowl with the hulls while extracting the large, round seeds. Use the back of a large spoon to get as much pulp as possible. Discard the seeds and transfer the hulls and pulp back to the saucepan. Cook them over medium heat to soften the hulls, 5 minutes more. Add the sugar mixture and lemon juice to the grapes and stir to mix everything well. Pour the filling into the piecrust. Sprinkle the small bits of butter over the grape filling, distributing it evenly. Wet the rim of the bottom piecrust, to help seal it.

(continued)

Roll the remaining dough into a 10-inch circle and cover the filling. Trim away the extra pastry extending beyond the rim of the pie pan. Crimp the edges firmly, or press them down with the back of a fork, working your way around the edge of the pie to seal the crust well. Use a sharp knife to cut eight slits in the top crust, to allow steam to escape and fruit juices to bubble up as the pie cooks.

Place the pie on a baking sheet to catch drips, and place it on the bottom shelf of the oven. Bake for 10 minutes, and then reduce the heat to 350 degrees F. Bake until the crust is a handsome, golden brown, and the grape juices are bubbling up through the crust, 35 to 45 minutes more.

Place the pie on a cooling rack or a folded kitchen towel and let cool for 10 minutes. Serve warm or at room temperature.

Blue Grass Cranberry Pie

MAKES ONE 9-INCH PIE

This lovely pie strikes me as an antique hidden in the attic, out of sight and therefore unappreciated despite its charms. Many turn-of-the-twentieth-century cookbooks include cranberry pies, with the fruit cooked to a thick jam before the cook puts them into a pastry crust. This one is from a treasure of African American culinary tradition and American history, *The Blue Grass Cook Book*. It pairs raw cranberries with raisins and cooks them completely in the pie, saving a step and delivering a delightful and beautiful dessert, perfect for holiday celebrations in every way. It's simple, it's traditional, it's unusual, it's beautiful and thematically red, and it's delicious. Not overly tangy, it's magnificent with ice cream or whipped cream. I've increased the proportion of cranberries, so that they outnumber the raisins to very nice effect. Use fresh cranberries during the holiday season when they are easy to find in the grocery store, but look for frozen cranberries if you don't see them in the produce section (use frozen cranberries directly from the freezer, without thawing).

PASTRY FOR A 9-INCH DOUBLE-CRUST PIE (STORE-BOUGHT OR SEE BASIC PIECRUSTS, PAGE 134)

I TABLESPOON BUTTER, SOFTENED

I TABLESPOON ALL-PURPOSE FLOUR

I CUP SUGAR

1½ CUPS (6 OUNCES) RAW CRANBERRIES

½ CUP (3 OUNCES) RAISINS

Heat the oven to 350 degrees F. Line a 9-inch pie pan with crust, leaving a ½-inch overhang (see page 138). Have the pastry for the top crust handy.

In a medium bowl, combine the butter and flour, and mash with a fork to mix them well and make a smooth paste. Add the sugar and continue mashing and mixing to combine everything into a crumbly mixture.

Add the cranberries and raisins, and toss and stir to mix everything together well. Pour the filling into the piecrust, and wet the top edge of the crust with a little water. Roll the remaining dough into a 10-inch circle and place it carefully over the filling. Fold the pastry extending beyond the rim of the pie pan up over the top crust, and press firmly to seal the bottom crust and the top crust together. Pinch the crust together firmly and crimp it to seal the edges; or go around the edges with the tines of a fork, pressing to seal the opening and make a handsome design as you work your way around the edge of the pie. Use a sharp knife to cut eight slits in the top of the pie, so that steam can escape and the filling can bubble up through the crust.

Place the pie on a baking sheet to catch drips, and place it on the middle shelf of the oven. Bake until the crust is golden brown, and the filling is bubbly and thick, 40 to 50 minutes. Place the pie on a cooling rack or a folded kitchen towel and let cool to room temperature.

Winchester Sun Pumpkin Pie

MAKES ONE 9-INCH PIE

To me, pumpkin pie is too fine to keep for holidays only. I love it for breakfast as well as on the holiday dessert line-up, and I love just about every version—plain or highly spiced, made with milk or luscious cream. There's plenty of room for suiting yourself with this pie, so keep your own counsel regarding spices. I'm partial to ginger and cloves, but you can use the spice mix known as "pumpkin pie spice," or a standard cinnamon-nutmeg combination, or simply leave it plain. It's a basic, flame-colored custard that has pleased us at the Southern table for several hundred years. I've adapted this standard pie from a recipe that appeared in Kentucky's the *Winchester Sun* newspaper in 1967. The spice list looks long, but it's a quick scoop with a tiny spoon, and the pie comes together fast.

PASTRY FOR A 9-INCH SINGLE-CRUST PIE (STORE-BOUGHT OR SEE BASIC PIECRUSTS, PAGE 134)

¾ CUP SUGAR

1 TEASPOON GROUND CINNAMON

½ TEASPOON GROUND GINGER

½ TEASPOON SALT

¼ TEASPOON GROUND NUTMEG

¼ TEASPOON GROUND CLOVES

2 CUPS PUMPKIN PUREE (TWO 15-OUNCE CANS; SEE NOTE)

¾ CUP EVAPORATED MILK

2 EGGS, BEATEN WELL

¼ CUP SORGHUM (SEE PAGE 154), PURE CANE SYRUP, OR HONEY

Heat the oven to 450 degrees F. Line a 9-inch pie pan with crust and then crimp the edges decoratively (see page 138).

In a small bowl, combine the sugar, cinnamon, ginger, salt, nutmeg, and cloves. Use a fork to stir everything together well. In a medium bowl, combine the pumpkin, milk, eggs, and sorghum. Use a fork, a whisk, or a large spoon to stir everything together, mixing it up into a thick, smooth filling. Add the sugar mixture and stir to mix it in and combine everything evenly and well.

Pour the filling into the piecrust and place it on the bottom shelf of the oven. Bake for 10 minutes, and then reduce the heat to 325 degrees F. Bake until the edges puff up and the center is fairly firm, wiggling only a little when you gently nudge the pan, 30 to 40 minutes. Place the pie on a cooling rack or a folded kitchen towel and let cool to room temperature.

NOTE: While I often find pleasure in doing something "from scratch" or in an old-timey way, I much prefer to use canned pumpkin in my pies. I love its dark color, creamy texture, and convenience. When I cook down fresh pumpkin, I'm always astounded by how watery it tends to be, even after multiple draining attempts. But both are good options. If you enjoy preparing pumpkin fresh, check farmers' markets for pumpkins cultivated for cooking, rather than for Halloween lanterns.

Persimmon Pie

MAKES ONE 9-INCH PIE

Wild persimmons still thrive in Southern soil, with spindly trees growing alongside fields and edging forests from the Piedmont to the Appalachian Mountains. I fell hard for persimmon pudding during my childhood, when square pans of it appeared at covered dish suppers and funeral feasts in the dwindling light of fall. A rustic confection, somewhere between cake, fudge, and pudding, persimmon pudding delivers the taste and colors of fall perfectly. While pudding is the most common recipe, persimmon pies are popular in parts of the South, made with less flour and more butter and milk.

Wild fall persimmons are magnificent, and worthy of the effort and cost to obtain and strain them; domesticated persimmons also work nicely in this pie (see Note). To obtain persimmon pulp, gather lots of very ripe, soft persimmons, and mash them through a colander to capture their pulp and relieve them of their astounding number of seeds. A food mill didn't work for me—the huge percentage of seeds brought the sturdy tool to its handheld knees. You'll make a big sticky mess while accumulating enough pulp, but I think you'll be glad you did once you've made your pie. The pulp freezes very well. Renowned chef Bill Smith, of Crook's Corner here in Chapel Hill, North Carolina, freezes lots of wild persimmon pulp so he can offer his delicious warm persimmon pudding well into the wintertime.

PASTRY FOR A 9-INCH SINGLE-CRUST PIE (STORE-BOUGHT OR SEE BASIC PIECRUSTS, PAGE 134)

I CUP SUGAR

2 TABLESPOONS ALL-PURPOSE FLOUR

½ TEASPOON GROUND CINNAMON

¼ TEASPOON GROUND NUTMEG

¼ TEASPOON SALT

¾ CUP EVAPORATED MILK

2 EGGS, BEATEN WELL

2 TABLESPOONS BUTTER, MELTED

I ½ CUPS PERSIMMON PULP

Heat the oven to 400 degrees F. Line a 9-inch pie pan with crust and then crimp the edges decoratively (see page 138).

In a small bowl, combine the sugar, flour, cinnamon, nutmeg, and salt. Stir with a fork to mix well. In a medium bowl, combine the milk, eggs, and butter, and stir with a whisk or a fork to combine them smoothly and well. Add the sugar mixture and stir to dissolve it into the custard. Add the persimmon pulp, and stir to combine everything evenly and well.

Pour the filling into the piecrust and place it on the middle shelf of the oven. Bake for 10 minutes. Reduce the heat to 350 degrees F and bake until the pie is fairly firm, shiny, and cracking around the edges, 30 to 40 minutes more.

Place the pie on a cooling rack or a folded kitchen towel and let cool for at least 45 minutes. Serve warm or at room temperature.

NOTE: You can use domesticated persimmons, both Hachiya and Fuyu varieties, for this pie. If the persimmon is firm, core it and then peel off the skin. If it is soft, cut it open, remove the stem portion, and scoop the moist pulp right off the skin from the inside. Either way, discard any seeds. Purée the pulp in a food processor or a blender and you're ready to go with your pie.

REGIONAL TREASURES FROM THE SEA ISLANDS to THE GREAT SMOKIES

Regional specialties invite us to savor a story about people, places, and points in time. Anchored by the ingredients that grew wild or were cultivated in a given place, and shaped by the traditions and preferences of their creators, regional dishes introduce us to the cultures that brought them to the table. Some recipes, like Key Lime Pie (page 106), arose from what grew easily and well in a given place. Others, like Cajun Tarte à la Bouillie (page 112) sprouted from affection for a distant homeland and took root in immigrant kitchens as a way to nurture memory and tradition.

Travel by pie in your mind's eye to Georgia's Sapelo Island, where heirloom pear trees sway in a sea breeze; or to an Appalachian mountain cabin, where soup beans bubble on the stove while families crack open black walnuts harvested each fall from one-hundred-year-old trees. Imagine an elegant dining room in New Orleans' French Quarter, Colonial Williamsburg's taverns, or a community living out its religious faith in every moment of daily life. From Sapelo Island Pear Pie (page 99) to Shaker Lemon Pie (page 103), and from Surry County Peach Sonker (page 101), to New Orleans Creole Coconut Pie (page 111), you can explore landscapes, languages, and seasons all around the South. Let these pies send you on a little journey, or inspire you to plan a real expedition to some delicious destination that comes to mind. Whether you travel in truth or in your mind, the trip will be sweeter if you take along a piece of pie.

Sapelo Island Pear Pie

MAKES ONE 9-INCH PIE

Descended from the Geechee people who settled on Sapelo Island in 1803, Mrs. Cornelia Walker Bailey proudly tends the fires of remembrance and history in the Sea Islands off the Georgia coast. A walking treasury of cultural traditions, she tells stories of courage and strength in *God, Dr. Buzzard and the Bolito Man: A Saltwater Geechee Talks about Life on Sapelo Island, Georgia*. Noting that living off the land was a necessity rather than an option, Mrs. Bailey recalls life in a "make-do society," including eating with the seasons. Her mother's pear pies were great treats, baked up for special occasions through the winter. She used quart jars of the pear preserves she had "put up" the previous fall when the pear trees of Sapelo Island were weighed down with fruit. Inspired by Mrs. Bailey's description, I cooked pears on the stove to make a preserve-like filling, and then baked into a pastry crust. You can use Bartlett pears, which have a handsome golden-brown skin and a pointy teardrop shape, or plump, green-skinned Anjou pears.

PASTRY FOR A 9-INCH DOUBLE-CRUST PIE (STORE-BOUGHT OR SEE BASIC PIECRUSTS, PAGE 134)

6 CUPS PEELED, CORED, AND CHOPPED PEARS (ABOUT 3 POUNDS)

¾ CUP PACKED DARK OR LIGHT BROWN SUGAR

½ CUP SUGAR

1½ TEASPOONS GROUND CINNAMON

1 TEASPOON GROUND NUTMEG

¼ TEASPOON GROUND CLOVES

3 TABLESPOONS BUTTER

2 TABLESPOONS ALL-PURPOSE FLOUR

Heat the oven to 375 degrees F. Line a 9-inch pie pan with crust, leaving a ½-inch overhang (see page 138).

In a large saucepan or Dutch oven, combine the pears, sugars, ¼ cup water, the cinnamon, nutmeg, and cloves. Bring to a gentle boil and then quickly reduce the heat to a lively simmer. Cook, stirring now and then to mix everything together, until the pears are tender and surrounded by a clear, fragrant syrup, 15 to 20 minutes. Remove from the heat, add the butter and the flour, and stir to mix everything well. Pour the pear filling into the piecrust.

Roll the remaining dough into a 10-inch circle and place it carefully over the filling. Trim away the extra pastry extending beyond the rim of the pie pan. Fold the crust up and over, and

crimp it decoratively. Or press the tines of a fork into the pastry rim, working around the pan to make a design. Use a sharp knife to make eight slits in the top of the pie, so that steam can escape and the pie's juices can bubble up.

Place the pie on a baking sheet to catch any drips and place it on the center shelf of the oven. Bake until the crust is golden brown and the filling bubbles up through the top of the pie, 40 to 50 minutes. Place the pie on a cooling rack or a folded kitchen towel and let cool for at least 45 minutes. Serve warm or at room temperature.

Surry County Peach Sonker with Dip

MAKES ONE 9-x-13-INCH SONKER

Situated between the city of Winston-Salem, North Carolina, and the Virginia state line, Surry County is a beautiful stretch of North Carolina Piedmont landscape. It has green, rolling hills, rich farmlands, apple and cherry orchards, and a view of Pilot Mountain nearby and the Blue Ridge Mountains on the western horizon. Great home cooks abound there, and while their expertise is broad, particular glory goes to one famous local dish, the Surry County Sonker. You might call it a deep-dish cobbler if you weren't from around there, and you might guess rightly that it comes from a long, proud tradition of serving local ingredients cooked into irresistible dishes for big, hungry crowds. Sonkers are made in the biggest pans cooks can find that still fit into a home oven, and they tend to have generous strips of pastry woven in a criss-cross or lattice fashion over the filling. Sweet potato sonkers are a particular favorite, especially on cold winter nights, but cooks have always adapted to what's fresh and in season, from blackberries and blueberries to strawberries, cherries, and peaches. This peach sonker is sparked with a little cinnamon, and paired with Surry County Sonker's particular finishing touch: dip. Whether served warm or at room temperature, sonkers call for the sweet, satisfying sauce known as "dip" that is poured over each serving. An everyday dip would be a milk-and-sugar sauce, and fancy would include an egg, making it akin to the classic Southern dessert sauce, boiled custard.

PASTRY FOR THREE 9-INCH SINGLE-CRUST PIES (STORE-BOUGHT OR SEE BASIC PIECRUSTS, PAGE 134)

FILLING
1½ CUPS SUGAR
⅓ CUP ALL-PURPOSE FLOUR

½ TEASPOONS GROUND CINNAMON
½ TEASPOON GROUND NUTMEG
½ TEASPOON SALT
9 CUPS PEELED AND CHOPPED FRESH OR FROZEN PEACHES, CUT INTO LARGE CHUNKS (3½ POUNDS)
½ CUP BUTTER, MELTED

DIP
½ CUP SUGAR
3 TABLESPOONS CORNSTARCH
3 CUPS MILK
½ TEASPOON VANILLA EXTRACT

Roll out half of the dough or use two pastry circles to line a 9-x-13-inch baking pan, tucking the dough into the corners. Press gently to seal up any seams if using two rounds of dough. Trim away excess dough to leave a 1-inch overhang.

Roll out the remaining dough and scraps and cut it into long strips 1 inch wide. To make a criss-cross pattern on top of the sonker, you will need six 14-inch-long strips, and twelve 10-inch long strips. Don't worry about perfection—you can piece together strips of dough as you go along to get enough to arrange over the fruit filling. Set the pastry-lined pan and dough strips aside while you prepare the filling. (You may have some extra dough. If so, simply wrap it airtight and freeze it for your next sonker or pie.)

Heat the oven to 450 degrees F.

(continued)

To make the filling: In a large bowl, combine the sugar, flour, cinnamon, nutmeg, and salt. Use a fork to stir everything together well. Add the peaches and gently stir and toss, until the fruit is evenly coated with the sugar mixture. Pour the filling into the pan and spread it out into an even layer. Pour the butter and ½ cup water evenly over the peaches.

Carefully arrange the 6 longer pastry strips on top of the peach filling, placing them evenly along the length of the pan, so that the filling shows through. Place the 12 shorter pastry strips at right angles to the long strips, arranging them along the width of the pan, to make a criss-cross pattern with peach filling showing through.

Press the end of each pastry strip firmly against the side of the pan, so that it sticks to the crust. Then fold the bottom edge of the pastry down and over the sealed strips, pressing it against the pastry-lined sides of the pan, going all the way around the rim of the pan. Crimp this crust edge by pinching it into little points, or press it with the tines of a fork to make a design.

Place the sonker on the middle shelf of the oven, and bake for 10 minutes. Lower the heat to 350 degrees F, and bake until the crust is handsomely and evenly browned, and the filling is bubbling up vigorously, 45 to 55 minutes more.

To make the dip: In a small or medium saucepan, combine the sugar and cornstarch and stir with a fork to mix them well. Add the milk and vanilla, and stir to dissolve the sugar mixture into the milk. Place the saucepan over medium-high heat, and stir as you let it come to a boil. As soon as the dip boils, reduce the heat so that it maintains a lively simmer, and cook, stirring often, until it thickens and is smooth, 3 to 5 minutes. Remove from the heat and set aside to cool.

Place the sonker on a cooling rack or a folded kitchen towel and let cool for 10 minutes. Serve warm or at room temperature, with a pitcher or a serving bowl and ladle of dip.

Shaker Lemon Pie

The Shakers, an early-nineteenth-century religious group who knew that good things like lemon pie were worth waiting for, lived and worked in communities throughout New England, and established a vibrant Shaker fellowship in Pleasant Hill, Kentucky. Preserved as a living history museum, today's Shaker Village at Pleasant Hill illuminates their traditions and creations, including woodworking, farming, spinning, and stonework. Their restaurants serve this signature confection, Shaker Lemon Pie.

For those of us who adore lemons, it is magnificent, and if you simply appreciate thrift and culinary creativity, you'll admire its unique approach. The issue is its pithy-ness. Shaker lemon pie uses the entire lemon, from yellow peel through white pith and all the way to the interior seeds. This means slicing two whole lemons absolutely paper thin, and macerating them for hours in sugar. The resulting pie includes a subtle sharp flavor from the pith, and the texture tends toward the chewy side, but it all works for the aforementioned lemon-lovers like myself. For my version, I chop the thinly sliced lemons coarsely, so that despite my uneven slicing, the lemon pieces are bite sized. I also add a little flour, to thicken the juices a bit. Plan ahead, so that you can set the mixture of very thinly sliced lemons and sugar aside for at least three hours and ideally, overnight. This makes for a softer texture and profoundly lemony flavor in your pie.

2 MEDIUM LEMONS

2 CUPS SUGAR

PASTRY FOR A 9-INCH DOUBLE-CRUST PIE (STORE-BOUGHT OR SEE BASIC PIECRUSTS, PAGE 134)

4 EGGS, BEATEN WELL

2 TABLESPOONS ALL-PURPOSE FLOUR

¼ TEASPOON SALT

Using your sharpest knife (a serrated knife is ideal), trim each lemon to remove the stem end and tip. Slice each lemon crosswise, as thinly as you can possibly do it, into paper-thin circles. If you can drape them over the knife blade like the watches in Salvador Dali's surrealistic paintings, you're on the right track. Scoop up as much of the escaping lemon juices as you can, and add them to the bowl of sliced lemons.

Chop the thinly sliced lemons coarsely, so that the largest pieces of lemon rind and pith are only 1 inch long, again gathering escaping juices back into the bowl for their flavor.

Add the sugar to the bowl of lemons, and stir to mix them together really well. Cover and set aside at room temperature, for at least 3 hours and as long as overnight. Stir occasionally with a big spoon, to mix everything together well.

(continued)

Heat the oven to 450 degrees F. Line a 9-inch pie pan with the crust, leaving a 1-inch overhang (see page 138).

Add the eggs, flour, and salt to the bowl of sugary lemons. Stir to mix everything evenly and well. Pour this filling into the piecrust.

Use a little water to wet the top rim of pastry around the piecrust. Roll the remaining dough into a 10-inch circle and place it carefully over the filling. Trim away the extra pastry, leaving a 1-inch overhang extending beyond the rim of the pie pan. Fold the crust up and over, and crimp it decoratively.

Or press the tines of a fork into the pastry rim, working around the pan to make a design. Cut eight steam vents in the top of the pie, so that steam can escape and the pie's juices can bubble up.

Place the pie on a baking sheet and place it on the middle shelf of the oven. Bake for 15 minutes. Reduce the heat to 375 degrees F and bake until the filling is bubbling and thickened, and the pastry crust is cooked and handsomely browned, 25 to 35 minutes more. Place the pie on a cooling rack or a folded kitchen towel and let cool to room temperature.

Key Lime Pie

MAKES ONE 9-INCH PIE

The classic Key lime pie always strikes me as a modern sort of confection, but it is a genuine old-timer, a pie that South Florida's people were devouring with glee back in the 1890s. Key limes are walnut-sized citrus fruits with an uneven yellow-green rind and a cool, pale green inner pulp. Though they thrive in the necklace of islands that make up the Florida Keys, Key limes are not from there. Most likely, they blew in long ago on trading ships, by way of South Asian ports of call.

The traditional Key lime pie is simple, elemental, and delicious. Sweetened condensed milk has been in the American pantry since the 1860s, and without pastureland nor dairy cows to provide milk, residents of the Keys took to it early on and spun it into a local specialty that the nation adores. The original Key lime pie called for a baked pastry crust, but graham cracker crusts were embraced as an early variation, and they are my favorite.

Look for Key limes in small net bags in the produce section seasonally, or order Key lime juice by mail (see page 156). Allow a little time for this pie. While it's one of the simplest to put together, the filling needs three hours to chill once it's made.

ONE 9-INCH GRAHAM CRACKER CRUST (STORE-BOUGHT OR SEE PAGE 134)

FILLING
4 EGG YOLKS
ONE 14-OUNCE CAN SWEETENED CONDENSED MILK (1¼ CUPS)
½ CUP KEY LIME JUICE (FROM 10 TO 15 LIMES), BOTTLED JUICE, OR REGULAR LIME JUICE
¼ TEASPOON SALT

TOPPING
1¼ CUPS HEAVY CREAM
3 TABLESPOONS CONFECTIONERS' SUGAR
1 TEASPOON VANILLA EXTRACT

Heat the oven to 350 degrees F. Line a 9-inch pie pan with the crust and then bake the crust as directed in the recipe.

To make the filling: In a medium bowl, combine the egg yolks and the milk. Use a whisk or fork to mix them together evenly and well. Add the lime juice and salt, and stir well until you have a smooth, thick filling.

Spoon the filling into the graham cracker crust. Place the pie on the middle shelf of the oven, and bake for 15 minutes, until the filling is set.

Place the pie on a cooling rack or a folded kitchen towel and let cool to room temperature. Cover loosely and refrigerate for at least 3 hours and as long as overnight.

To make the topping: Whip the cream in a medium bowl. When it thickens and increases in volume, add the sugar and vanilla, and continue beating until the cream is billowing and thick, able to hold soft peaks beautifully and easily. Pile the whipped cream onto the pie filling. Refrigerate for 1 hour or more before serving. Serve cold.

Black Walnut Pie

MAKES ONE 9-INCH PIE

A close cousin of the hickory tree, black walnut trees are native to the United States, particularly throughout the Appalachian Mountains and into the Midwest. The town of Spencer has been hosting the West Virginia Black Walnut Festival each October since 1954, celebrating the tree that is prized for its beautiful wood as well as its rich, smoky-flavored nutmeats. The shells are extraordinarily difficult to crack, and the process stains hands and clothing, but Southern cooks have persevered for centuries to obtain an annual supply for use in making cakes, pies, ice cream, and fudge. These days, shelled black walnuts are widely available in supermarkets around the country, or check mail-order sources (see page 156).

PASTRY FOR ONE 9-INCH SINGLE-CRUST PIE (STORE-BOUGHT OR SEE BASIC PIECRUSTS, PAGE 134)

3 EGGS, BEATEN WELL

¾ CUP PACKED DARK OR LIGHT BROWN SUGAR

1 CUP SORGHUM, MOLASSES, OR DARK CORN SYRUP

½ CUP MELTED BUTTER

1 TEASPOON VANILLA EXTRACT

¼ TEASPOON SALT

1½ CUPS (6 OUNCES) CHOPPED BLACK WALNUTS

Heat the oven to 400 degrees F. Line a 9-inch pie pan with crust and then crimp the edges decoratively (see page 138). Line and partially bake the crust (see page 139).

In a medium bowl, combine the eggs and sugar. Use a fork or a whisk to mix them together evenly and well. Add the sorghum, butter, vanilla, and salt, and stir to combine them into a thick, smooth filling. Add the walnuts and stir to mix everything well. Pour the filling into the prepared piecrust.

Place the pie on the middle shelf of the oven. Bake for 10 minutes, and then reduce the heat to 350 degrees F. Bake until the edges puff up and the center is fairly firm, wiggling only a little when you gently nudge the pan.

Place the pie on a cooling rack or a folded kitchen towel and let cool to room temperature.

Mountain Home Soup Bean Pie

MAKES ONE 9-INCH PIE

From the Blue Ridge Mountains across the southern regions of the Appalachian mountain chain, home cooks rely on imagination and inspiration, making the most of what they grow, gather in the wild, and buy in the country store. Pinto beans are a nutritious, economical, and satisfying staple, easy to grow, cook, and keep. Paired with eggs and butter from home, and canned milk, sugar, and some spices from the store, pinto beans can move from being a substantial and savory main course to a sweet and satisfying treat.

PASTRY FOR A 9-INCH SINGLE-CRUST PIE (STORE-BOUGHT OR SEE BASIC PIECRUSTS, PAGE 134)

½ CUP GRANULATED SUGAR

½ CUP PACKED LIGHT OR DARK BROWN SUGAR

½ CUP EVAPORATED MILK, HALF-AND-HALF, OR MILK

½ CUP BUTTER, MELTED

2 EGGS, BEATEN WELL

1 TEASPOON VANILLA EXTRACT

½ TEASPOON GROUND CINNAMON

¼ TEASPOON SALT

1½ CUPS (ONE 15-OUNCE CAN) COOKED, DRAINED, PINTO BEANS (SEE NOTE)

Heat the oven to 375 degrees F. Line a 9-inch pie pan with crust and then crimp the edges decoratively (see page 138).

In a medium bowl, combine the sugars, milk, butter, eggs, vanilla, cinnamon, and salt. Use a whisk or a fork to mix everything well.

Mash the beans well, and press them through a colander to remove some of the husks. Add to the milk mixture and stir with a whisk or a large spoon, to combine everything evenly and well.

Pour the filling into the piecrust and place it on the bottom rack of the oven. Bake for 10 minutes, and then reduce the heat to 325 degrees F. Bake until the filling is firm and handsomely browned, about 35 minutes more. Place the pie on a cooling rack or a folded kitchen towel and let cool for 10 minutes. Serve warm or at room temperature.

NOTE: Use unseasoned canned beans for this pie, not spicy or highly seasoned ones.

New Orleans Creole Coconut Pie

MAKES ONE 9-INCH PIE

For endless and delicious tastes of history, open up *The Picayune Creole Cook Book*, first published by the New Orleans newspaper the *Picayune* in 1900. Among more than three dozen recipes for pies and pastry are two coconut pies—one a standard coconut custard pie, and a *Tarte de Coco à la Creole*. Here is my version of the latter, a traditional confection that is a pleasure to make and to eat. The amount of nutmeg (a tablespoonful) is generous, and while it suits me just fine, do adjust it according to your taste. While I have no reason to think that the originators of this lovely pie did so, I love to serve this pie with a spoonful of sweetened berries or whipped cream sweetened with blackberry or raspberry jam.

PASTRY FOR A 9-INCH SINGLE-CRUST PIE (STORE-BOUGHT OR SEE BASIC PIECRUSTS, PAGE 134)

2 CUPS MILK

1½ CUPS CONFECTIONERS' SUGAR

2 TABLESPOONS BUTTER, MELTED

¾ CUP WHITE WINE, APPLE JUICE, OR WHITE GRAPE JUICE

1 TABLESPOON GROUND NUTMEG

2 TEASPOONS VANILLA EXTRACT

2 CUPS SHREDDED, FLAKED, OR FRESHLY GRATED COCONUT, SWEETENED OR UNSWEETENED

6 EGG WHITES

Heat the oven to 350 degrees F. Line a 9-inch pie pan with crust and then crimp the edges decoratively (see page 138). Line and partially bake the crust (see page 139).

In a medium saucepan over medium heat, scald the milk by heating it until bubbles appear around the edges and the milk begins to steam; don't let it come to a boil. Remove from the heat and set it aside to cool to room temperature. (To speed things a bit, transfer the hot milk into a bowl or a large pitcher so that it will cool off more quickly than it would in the pan.)

In a medium bowl, combine 1 cup of the sugar and the butter and stir with a whisk or a large spoon to mix them together well. Add the wine, nutmeg, and vanilla, and stir well. Add the coconut and the cooled milk, and stir gently to mix them in well.

In a large bowl, using a whisk or an electric mixer, beat the egg whites until they become thick and airy and will hold stiff but still curly peaks. Add the egg whites into the bowl of coconut filling, folding them into the mixture as delicately as possible, so that the filling is light and puffed up. Quickly turn the coconut filling into the piecrust and spread it out delicately to fill the crust and seal the edges.

Place the pie on the bottom rack of the oven and bake until the filling is puffed, fairly firm, and delicately brown, about 30 minutes.

Place the pie on a cooling rack or a folded kitchen towel and let cool to room temperature. Just before serving, sprinkle the remaining ½ cup sugar over the top of the pie, like a sudden little flurry of snow, and serve.

Cajun Tarte à la Bouillie

MAKES ONE 9-INCH PIE

This pie is Cajun-country comfort food, pure and simple, baked up by generations of home cooks to the delight of children and grandchildren, new neighbors, elected officials, and parish priests—anyone lucky enough to be at the table in the South Louisiana countryside. Its French roots are clear, but in the hands of Louisiana's Cajun home cooks, the crust softened into sweet dough, a lovely egg-enriched pastry with a cookie-like quality. Sweet dough is made there into turnovers, cherished handheld treats filled with custard, fig jam, sweet potatoes, or sweetened seasonal fruit. The word *bouillie* means "boiled," a reference to the filling, a version of boiled custard that has been enjoyed as a sauce, a beverage, and a pastry filling throughout the South since colonial times. Tarte à la Bouillie comes in double-crust and lattice-top versions, and some are made with just one oversize sheet of dough that is folded loosely back in over the custard, nearly enclosing the luscious filling.

Check out bake sales, feast days, church suppers, First Communion celebrations, family reunions, *fais do dos*, and *boucheries* if you want to try this dessert, or head to a Rouse's Market in Louisiana or Mississippi. As a modern regional grocer with roots in Thibodeaux, Louisiana, Rouse's keeps Tarte à la Bouillie on their bakeshop menu fresh every day, because they want their customers to know, remember, and cherish the tastes of home.

SWEET DOUGH CRUST
2 CUPS ALL-PURPOSE FLOUR

⅓ CUP SUGAR

2 TEASPOONS BAKING POWDER

¼ TEASPOON SALT

¼ CUP BUTTER, CUT INTO ½-INCH CHUNKS

I EGG

I TEASPOON VANILLA EXTRACT

CUSTARD FILLING
3 CUPS MILK

¾ CUP SUGAR

¼ CUP CORNSTARCH

¼ TEASPOON SALT

3 EGGS, BEATEN WELL

3 TABLESPOONS BUTTER

I TEASPOON VANILLA EXTRACT

½ TEASPOON GROUND NUTMEG

To make the crust: In a medium bowl, combine the flour, sugar, baking powder, and salt, and stir with a fork to mix well. Add the butter and cut it into the flour mixture, using a pastry blender or your hands, mashing gently just enough to make a crumbly mixture with lots of small bits of butter still distinct.

In a small bowl, combine the egg with the vanilla and 3 tablespoons of cold water, and stir with a fork to mix them well. Pour the egg into the flour mixture, and stir gently with a spoon to bring everything together into a soft dough. Add more water (2 or 3 tablespoons) if you need it to make the ingredients come together. Shape the dough into a large ball, wrap in waxed paper, and flatten it gently into a large disk. Refrigerate for at least 1 hour.

To make the filling: Scald the milk by heating it in a medium saucepan until bubbles appear around the edges and the milk begins to steam; don't let it come to a boil. Remove it from the heat and set aside. In a medium bowl, combine the sugar, cornstarch, and salt. Stir with a whisk or a fork to combine well. Add the eggs and beat to mix everything well.

While stirring the egg mixture, slowly pour about ½ cup of the hot milk into the bowl. Stir well to warm up the eggs without scrambling them in the heat. Mix well, and then gently add another ⅓ cup of hot milk.

Pour the warmed egg mixture into the saucepan of milk and stir well. Return it to the stove and cook over low heat, stirring often and well to prevent sticking and burning, until the ingredients thicken into a nice, rich custard filling, 15 to 20 minutes. Add the butter, vanilla, and nutmeg, and stir to mix everything well. Remove it from the heat and set aside.

To finish making the dough, divide it into two parts, one large (two thirds of the dough) and one small (one third of the dough). Place the large part on a piece of waxed paper or parchment paper dusted lightly with flour. Dust the top of the dough with flour and place a second piece of waxed paper on top. Roll it into a 10-inch round. Carefully transfer the round to a 9-inch pie pan, and fit it in carefully. Roll out the smaller piece of dough between waxed paper, to make an 8-inch circle. Cut this dough into strips, about ¾ inch wide. Refrigerate the crust until you are ready to fill and bake the pie.

Heat the oven to 350 degrees F.

Pour the custard filling into the prepared piecrust. Arrange the strips of pastry over the custard in a criss-cross fashion, pressing each end of the pastry firmly against the edge of the bottom crust. Fold the edges of the crust up over the strips, enclosing them and forming a crust around the pie. Crimp this folded edge in a pointed design, or press it firmly with the back tines of a fork, making a parallel design.

Place the pie on the middle rack of the oven. Bake until the crust has puffed up a little and is handsomely and lightly browned, 30 to 35 minutes.

Place the pie on a cooling rack or a folded kitchen towel and let cool to room temperature.

Williamsburg Peanut Butter Cream Pie

MAKES ONE 9-INCH PIE

My friend and fellow food writer Paula LaMont clearly remembers her first visit to Colonial Williamsburg when she was but a child of six. The entire living-history experience captivated her, but the sweetest memory she has is her first taste of peanut butter cream pie. As Linda notes, "My mother knew what she was doing, spooning history down with this velvety Southern treat!" Williamsburg's Shield's Tavern has a luscious peanut butter pie on the menu today, celebrating one of Virginia's signature crops. Since Oregon-based Paula can't get to Williamsburg as often as she would like, she worked out her own version—one that has already gone down in history as a fine and worthy pie. Paula's chocolate cookie crust complements the pie perfectly, but either a graham cracker crumb crust or a fully baked pastry crust would work just fine.

CHOCOLATE COOKIE CRUST
1½ CUPS CRUSHED CHOCOLATE
WAFER COOKIES

½ CUP BUTTER, MELTED

½ CUP SUGAR

FILLING
½ CUP SUGAR

⅓ CUP CORNSTARCH

2 CUPS MILK

3 EGG YOLKS

½ CUP CREAMY PEANUT BUTTER

2 TEASPOONS VANILLA EXTRACT

TOPPING
1 CUP HEAVY CREAM

1 TABLESPOON CONFECTIONERS' SUGAR

1 TEASPOON VANILLA EXTRACT

¾ CUP (4 OUNCES) COARSELY CHOPPED,
DRY-ROASTED, SALTED PEANUTS

To make the crust: Heat the oven to 350 degrees F.

Combine the crushed cookies, butter, and sugar in the work bowl of a food processor, and pulse to blend them together well. Press the crumb crust mixture evenly into a greased 9-inch pie pan. Bake the crust for 10 minutes, and then set aside to cool. (You could also make cookie crumbs by hand, breaking or chopping the cookies coarsely, placing them in a sturdy plastic bag, and going over them with a rolling pin until you have fine crumbs.)

To make the filling: In a small bowl, combine the sugar and cornstarch using a fork or a whisk to mix them together evenly. In a medium saucepan, combine the milk and egg yolks, and stir well. Add the sugar mixture to the egg yolks and stir to mix them well. Cook over medium heat, stirring constantly, until the filling is thick and smooth, 10 to 12 minutes. Transfer it to a medium bowl and set aside to cool.

When the custard has cooled to room temperature, use a whisk or an electric mixer to beat it until creamy and thickened. Add the peanut butter and vanilla, beating well until everything is evenly combined. Scrape the filling into the baked piecrust, smoothing the surface to even it out. Cover and refrigerate until cold and firm.

To make the topping: Combine the cream and sugar in a medium bowl, and whip it using an electric mixer on high speed, or a whisk. When it has thickened enough to hold stiff peaks, beat in the vanilla, and then cover the peanut butter filling with the whipped cream. Smooth it out into a thick, even layer, sealing off the edges, and sprinkle the chopped peanuts over the top. Serve cold.

Pecan Chiffon Pie

MAKES ONE 9-INCH PIE

My friend Jean Anderson is a distinguished member of the James Beard Cookbook Hall of Fame, so anytime she publishes a new book, it's great news for cooks and food lovers alike. Her latest is a treasure on every level, especially for those many fans of the food, cooking, and cultural history of the South. *A Love Affair with Southern Cooking* captured the 2008 James Beard Best Cookbook Award in the category of Americana, and is a must for cooks, eaters, and readers. I'm so pleased that she shared this wonderful pie recipe with me, along with its story:

"Back when I was an Assistant Home Demonstration Agent in Iredell County, North Carolina (my first job out of college), I'd go to Charlotte on weekends. Compared to the little town of Statesville, where I lived, Charlotte was Big Time—the largest city in the state. It still is. I'd drive down to buy clothes, to see first-run movies, and also to eat. But not at fancy restaurants. I loved the lunch counter at Kress's five-and-ten-cent store (now gone, alas). And all because of the heavenly pecan chiffon pie served there. It was baked locally, perhaps even at the store, and its recipe was kept secret. In an effort to 'crack' it, I downed God knows how many pieces of Kress's pecan chiffon pie over the years. My flavor memories of it remain strong and this, my latest rendition, approximates the original."

PASTRY FOR A 9-INCH SINGLE-CRUST PIE (STORE-BOUGHT; SEE NOTE, OR SEE BASIC PIECRUSTS, PAGE 134)

FILLING

1 CUP (ABOUT 4 OUNCES) COARSELY CHOPPED, LIGHTLY TOASTED PECANS

2 TABLESPOONS PASTEURIZED EGG WHITE POWDER (SEE NOTE)

¾ CUP HEAVY CREAM

¾ CUP PACKED LIGHT BROWN SUGAR

3 TABLESPOONS CORNSTARCH

2½ TEASPOONS UNFLAVORED GELATIN

¼ TEASPOON SALT

1 TEASPOON VANILLA EXTRACT

TOPPING

1 CUP HEAVY CREAM

2 TABLESPOONS CONFECTIONERS' SUGAR

½ TEASPOON VANILLA EXTRACT

Heat the oven to 350 degrees F. Line a 9-inch pie pan with crust and then crimp the edges decoratively (see page 138). Line and fully bake the crust (see page 139).

To make the filling: Spread the pecans in a pie pan or on a baking sheet and toast them until they are fragrant and nicely browned, 10 to 12 minutes. Tip out onto a plate to cool. In a medium bowl, combine the pasteurized egg white powder and 6 tablespoons cold water and stir with a fork to combine them well. Set aside, while the mixture thickens.

In a medium, heavy saucepan, combine the cream, brown sugar, ½ cup cold water, the cornstarch, gelatin, and salt. Set aside until the gelatin softens, about 5 minutes.

Place the saucepan over medium heat, and bring the brown sugar mixture to a boil. Cook, stirring constantly, until thickened, about 3 minutes. Remove from the heat, stir in the vanilla, and set aside to cool until the mixture begins to set, 15 to 20 minutes.

Using an electric mixer on high speed, beat the egg white mixture until stiff peaks form, 2 to 3 minutes. Stir in the cooled brown sugar mixture, using a whisk or a large spoon, and then fold in the toasted pecans. Scoop the filling into the baked piecrust, smoothing the surface and spreading the filling all the way to the edge. Cover with an inverted pie pan or plastic wrap and refrigerate until firm, 2 to 3 hours.

To serve, prepare the topping: In a medium bowl, combine the cream, confectioners' sugar, and vanilla, and beat on high speed until the cream forms soft peaks. Swirl the whipped cream lavishly over the pecan filling, mounding it up nicely in the center. Serve at once, or refrigerate until serving time.

NOTE: If using a frozen piecrust shell, look for a deep-dish version.

Jean Anderson writes: "In the '50s and '60s when I was so smitten with this pie, it would have been made with egg whites beaten to great heights. There was no salmonella problem then and raw eggs weren't off-limits. Today there is and they are, so I've taken the liberty of substituting Just Whites, a pasteurized egg white powder sold at many supermarkets."

CHOCOLATE PIES

O f all the precious pies that Southern people hold dear, those made with chocolate are among the newer ones to arrive at the party. By this I don't mean that chocolate pies came in talking on their cell phones or by way of e-mail. *The Blue Grass Cook Book*, published in Kentucky in 1904, sets forth two lovely chocolate pies—one a classic chocolate pie with meringue on top, and the other a luscious chocolate custard made in a double crust and served with whipped cream. The same book includes a veritable fountain of chocolate in other forms, including a chocolate layer cake, three versions of hot chocolate, one steamed chocolate pudding, four chocolate custards, chocolate éclairs, chocolate ice cream, and a round-up of candy including chocolate caramels, chocolate drops, chocolate egg kisses, and chocolate fudge. Why not more chocolate in the form of pie, I am wondering?

Chocolate knowledge and appreciation was out there, as evidenced by author and food historian Damon Lee Fowler in his essential and fascinating, *Classical Southern Cooking: A Celebration of the Cuisine of the Old South*. He provides a wonderful and still workable recipe for Mary Randolph's Chocolate Custard Ice Cream from her 1824 cookbook, *The Virginia House-Wife*. Clearly chocolate was in the Southern kitchen and on the table going on two hundred years ago, so why was it so seldom employed in pies? While I pursue answers to that question, may I suggest you use your time wisely by sampling some of the fabulous chocolate pies that the Southern culinary repertoire does contain—some old and some new.

My favorite is the one I remember from my grandmother's kitchen—classic chocolate pie. I never got her recipe, but thank heavens my good friend and fellow food writer Linda Gilbert didn't make the same mistake. She got her Mama Irene's Chocolate Meringue Pie (page 122) down on paper, so that we can return it to the mainstream and keep it going for the next generation of Southern pie fans. Next come two winners, Chocolate Chess Pie (page 121) and Chocolate-Pecan Pie (page 124), each so simple to make and so rewarding, whether

(continued)

warm or room temperature, served with whipped cream, ice cream, or perfectly plain. If you're feeling ready for a chocolate project, you couldn't do better than to make a Black Bottom Pie (page 129). This nearly one-hundred-year-old treasure makes people swoon with pleasure, and if it was easier to make, we might all be eating it twice a week and not be the better for doing so. It's a kitchen challenge, not for difficulty, but simply because there's some cooking and some timing, and a number of steps to keep straight. It's a perfect recipe for a group project. Ring up your friends, and suggest a "Black Bottom Pie and a Movie" date, whereby you gather with the ingredients and an afternoon, and make the pie together, watching a movie or taking a nature walk during the down times. Then feast on your creation, or make a batch of pies so everybody has one to take home for later.

Chocolate Angel Pie (page 127) is a meringue cloud, calling for quite some time to bake and chill and fill, but it's simple, unusual, and a sure sensation at a celebration of any kind. Then there's German Chocolate Pie (page 125), my favorite pie from the K&W Cafeteria since I was not even eye-level to the display. It's velvety and crunchy—right at the magical intersection of coconut, chocolate, and pecans. Closing out the category is Tar Heel Pie (page 131). You may read somewhere that it is an old, classic North Carolina recipe, but take it from an old, classic North Carolina gal: This is not an heirloom recipe, and its history, such as it is, most likely doesn't dip too deeply back into the twentieth century. What it IS, is really, really good. It's too easy for words; too luscious to keep in the house unless you are better than me at hiding things from yourself. This is a good traveler, so I suggest you make it, take it whole and uncut to your celebration destination, and cut the first piece for you and set it out. You will not need to worry about dealing with any Tar Heel Pie to take home.

Now that's a very fine line-up of Southern pies of the chocolate variety, but I still think there's work to do. Let me send you out to make some of these pies, and then to come up with the next round of Southern-inspired chocolate pies. That way, this genre can catch up with coconut, lemon, and all the other Southern pie persuasions.

Chocolate Chess Pie

MAKES ONE 9-INCH PIE

Betty Thomason is a mighty fine home cook who knows how to make pies that please. Her chocolate chess pie delights her family and friends, and if you make one you will understand why. I adore it served just a bit warm, but that may be an issue of impatience, not wanting to give it time to cool all the way down after baking. I wouldn't heat it back up, as it is divine at room temperature, but I do firmly believe that when it is served almost daily in heaven, it comes with a side of whipped cream.

PASTRY FOR A 9-INCH SINGLE-CRUST PIE (STORE-BOUGHT OR SEE BASIC PIECRUSTS, PAGE 134)

½ CUP BUTTER

I SQUARE (I OUNCE) UNSWEETENED CHOCOLATE

I CUP SUGAR

2 EGGS, BEATEN WELL

I TEASPOON VANILLA EXTRACT

¼ TEASPOON SALT

Heat the oven to 325 degrees F. Line a 9-inch pie pan with crust and then crimp the edges decoratively (see page 138). Refrigerate it until needed.

Combine the butter and chocolate in a small saucepan over medium heat. Cook, stirring often, until the chocolate and butter melt and you can stir them together into a smooth sauce, 5 to 7 minutes. Remove from the heat, add the sugar, and stir well. Add the eggs, vanilla, and salt, and stir to combine everything evenly and well.

Pour the filling into the piecrust and place the pie on the bottom shelf of the oven. Bake until the pie is puffed up, fairly firm, and handsomely browned, 35 to 45 minutes.

Place the pie on a cooling rack or a folded kitchen towel and let cool for at least 10 minutes. Serve warm or at room temperature.

MAMA IRENE'S
Chocolate Meringue Pie

MAKES ONE 9-INCH PIE

My friend Linda Weiss has earned her stripes as a chef, cookbook author, and cooking teacher, but she considers grandmother "Mama Irene's" kitchen to be the place where her culinary career began. A school teacher and a mother, Mama Irene raised chickens and milked a cow, churned her own butter, and either cooked up or canned what came out of the garden. She was particularly famous for her fried chicken, which she brined before seasoning and frying it, and for her old-timey chocolate pie with meringue on top. Linda keeps Mama Irene's butter churn in her Charleston, South Carolina, kitchen, using it to hold her collection of rolling pins handy and ready for action. She also cherishes Mama Irene's chocolate pie recipe, which she kindly shared with me so that I could pass it along to you.

PASTRY FOR A 9-INCH SINGLE-CRUST PIE (STORE-BOUGHT OR SEE BASIC PIECRUSTS, PAGE 134)

FILLING

I CUP SUGAR

½ CUP COCOA

3 TABLESPOONS CORNSTARCH

¼ TEASPOON SALT

2 CUPS MILK

3 EGG YOLKS

I TEASPOON VANILLA EXTRACT

MERINGUE

3 EGG WHITES

6 TABLESPOONS SUGAR

Line a 9-inch pie pan with crust and then crimp the edges decoratively (see page 138). Line and fully bake the crust (see page 139). Set it aside to cool.

To make the filling: In a medium bowl, combine the sugar, cocoa, cornstarch, and salt, and stir with a fork to mix well.

In a medium saucepan, combine the milk and egg yolks. Stir with a fork to mix well.

Add the sugar-cocoa mixture to the saucepan, and use a fork to mix well.

Place over medium-high heat. Cook, stirring often, until the mixture comes to a gentle boil. Reduce the heat to medium and continue cooking, stirring and scraping the sides and bottom of the pan often, until the filling becomes shiny and thickens to a silky, rich texture, 3 to 5 minutes. Stir in the vanilla and pour the filling into the baked piecrust. Set aside at room temperature while you prepare the meringue.

Heat the oven to 325 degrees F.

To make the meringue: In a large bowl, beat the egg whites with an electric mixer on medium speed until foamy. Increase the speed to high, and beat until the egg whites begin to thicken to the texture of cream. Add the sugar 2 tablespoons at a time, beating well each time, until the meringue is thick, shiny, and able to hold curly firm peaks. Spread the meringue evenly over the cooked pie filling, sealing the edges to the crust completely and then piling the egg whites higher in the center of the pie. Use a spoon to form curly peaks all over the meringue.

Place the pie in the oven and bake until the meringue is handsomely golden brown, 10 to 15 minutes. Cool to room temperature and serve.

Chocolate-Pecan Pie

MAKES ONE 9-INCH PIE

Simply luscious and rich, but not hard to make at all, this pie is a modern favorite. It's a good choice when you need a make-ahead, take-along dessert. Let it come to room temperature before serving if it has been refrigerated for more than two hours. I would consider a generous dollop of whipped cream or a scoop of vanilla ice cream to be worthy accompaniments for this decadent pie.

PASTRY FOR A 9-INCH SINGLE-CRUST PIE (STORE-BOUGHT OR SEE BASIC PIECRUSTS, PAGE 134)

½ CUP BUTTER

3 SQUARES (3 OUNCES) UNSWEETENED CHOCOLATE

1 CUP SUGAR

¾ CUP DARK OR LIGHT CORN SYRUP

4 EGGS, BEATEN WELL

1 TEASPOON VANILLA EXTRACT

¼ TEASPOON SALT

1½ CUPS (6 OUNCES) COARSELY CHOPPED PECANS

Heat the oven to 350 degrees F. Line a 9-inch pie pan with crust and then crimp the edges decoratively (see page 138).

In a medium saucepan, combine the butter and chocolate over medium heat. Cook, stirring often, until the chocolate and butter melt and you can stir them together into a smooth sauce, 5 to 7 minutes.

Remove from the heat and add the sugar and corn syrup. Stir to combine well. Add the eggs, vanilla, and salt, and stir to mix everything together into a thick, smooth chocolate filling. Add the pecans, stir well, and pour the filling into the piecrust.

Place the pie on the bottom rack of the oven. Bake until the filling puffs up and is fairly firm in the middle, 30 to 40 minutes.

Place the pie on a cooling rack or a folded kitchen towel, and let cool to room temperature.

FRED THOMPSON'S

German Chocolate Pie

MAKES ONE 9-INCH PIE

My friend and fellow food writer Fred Thompson came up with this recipe to please his mom, a superb Southern cook who wasn't quite sure her son knew his way around a kitchen. Now she knows, and you can be sure you'll please anyone on your list with it. My favorite pie on the K&W Cafeteria dessert shelves since childhood, this substantial confection is deep chocolate velvet custard heaven, with a crunchy coconut-pecan top. Fred uses Baker's German Sweet Chocolate as his semisweet chocolate of choice in his version, featured in his must-have *Big Book of Fish and Shellfish*.

Bless the insightful baker who first mused on the idea of translating German chocolate cake into pie form. With coconut and chopped pecans forming a crunchy-sweet layer over the velvety milk-chocolate filling, this pie echoes several classic pies as well as its cake inspiration with spectacular results.

PASTRY FOR A 9-INCH SINGLE-CRUST DEEP-DISH PIE (STORE-BOUGHT OR SEE BASIC PIECRUSTS, PAGE 134)

1½ CUPS (ABOUT 6 OUNCES) SHREDDED SWEETENED COCONUT

1 CUP (4 OUNCES) CHOPPED PECANS

4 SQUARES (4 OUNCES) SEMISWEET OR BITTERSWEET CHOCOLATE

¼ CUP BUTTER

1¼ CUPS EVAPORATED MILK OR HALF-AND-HALF

1½ CUPS SUGAR

3 TABLESPOONS CORNSTARCH

½ TEASPOON SALT

2 EGGS, LIGHTLY BEATEN

1 TEASPOON VANILLA EXTRACT

Heat the oven to 375 degrees F. Line a 9-inch deep-dish pie pan with crust and then crimp the edges decoratively (see page 138).

Combine the coconut and pecans in a medium bowl and mix them well.

Break up or chop the chocolate into small chunks. Combine it with the butter in a medium saucepan and cook over medium-low heat until melted, swirling the pan to help things along. Add the milk, stir well, and set aside. (It will not be smooth, and that's fine.)

In a medium bowl, combine the sugar, cornstarch, and salt, and use a fork or a whisk to combine them evenly. Add the eggs and vanilla and stir to combine everything well. Scrape it into the chocolate mixture, and stir well. Pour this fairly smooth, thick chocolate filling into the pie shell. Sprinkle the coconut-pecan mixture evenly over the top.

Place the pie on the lower shelf of the oven. Bake until the filling is puffed up, lightly browned, and fairly firm, 45 to 50 minutes. Place the pie on a cooling rack or a folded kitchen towel and let cool to room temperature. Cover and refrigerate until shortly before serving time. Serve lightly chilled or at room temperature.

Chocolate Angel Pie

MAKES ONE 9-INCH PIE

This delicate dessert is an ethereal pie, in which meringue—usually pie's accessory—becomes the crust. Like the Pavlova of Australia and New Zealand, angel pie features a large meringue as the main event. But while Pavlovas are usually filled with sweetened fruit, angel pies are typically filled with lemon curd and whipped cream, or a simple chocolate mousse. Both angel pies and Pavlovas are iterations of the classic Viennese *schaum torte*. Some Southern cooks add pecans to the meringue crust, making the angel-cloud base quite reminiscent of Divinity, a classic Southern candy. Around the South, angel pies are cherished throughout the year as a celestial party dish.

MERINGUE CRUST
4 EGG WHITES
¼ TEASPOON CREAM OF TARTAR
⅛ TEASPOON SALT
¾ CUP SUGAR

½ TEASPOON VANILLA EXTRACT
½ CUP (2 OUNCES) CHOPPED PECANS

CHOCOLATE CREAM FILLING
4 SQUARES (4 OUNCES) SEMISWEET CHOCOLATE

I TEASPOON VANILLA EXTRACT
I CUP HEAVY CREAM

SWEETENED WHIPPED CREAM AND COCOA POWDER, FOR GARNISH (OPTIONAL)

To make the meringue crust: Heat the oven to 275 degrees F. Lightly grease a 9-inch pie pan and set aside.

In a medium bowl with an electric mixer, beat the egg whites until they are bubbly and foamy. Add the cream of tartar and salt, and beat on high speed until the egg whites begin to swell up and hold their shape. Add the sugar gradually, and then the vanilla, while you continue to beat the egg whites, until they are thick, light, shiny, and able to hold firm, curled peaks.

Scoop the beaten egg whites out into the pie plate and use the back of a large spoon to shape them into a piecrust with high sides, extending a little above the sides of the pie pan. Scatter the chopped pecans over the bottom of the meringue crust.

Place the pan on the middle shelf of the oven. Bake for 10 minutes. Lower the temperature to 250 degrees F, and bake until the meringue crust is lightly browned, firm, and dry to the touch, 45 to 50 minutes more.

Place the pan on a cooling rack or a folded kitchen towel and let cool to room temperature. Then refrigerate the crust for 3 hours, until very cold.

To make the filling: Melt the chocolate in a small saucepan over medium-low heat. Add ¼ cup hot water and the vanilla and stir well to combine everything smoothly. Set aside to cool completely.

When the chocolate is cool, beat the cream until it is thick and light and holds firm peaks. Gently stir the whipped cream into the chocolate and fold them together to make a delicate, creamy chocolate filling.

Scoop the chocolate filling into the meringue piecrust and mound it up handsomely. Refrigerate it for 3 hours or more and serve cold, with extra whipped cream and a cocoa powder dusting, if you like.

Black Bottom Pie

MAKES ONE 9-INCH PIE

With a layer of chocolate topped by a layer of custard, and crowned with whipped cream, this pie has dazzled Southerners for almost one hundred years. It takes some time to stir up its various components, but the result of your efforts will be a spectacular dessert. None of the steps is particularly difficult, but there are lots of details that need your attention (see Note), so make this when you're ready to invest some time in return for dazzling results.

The top layer of custard gets a lift from stiffly beaten egg whites, which go into the custard uncooked. You can use powdered egg whites (see Note) for this step. Whipped cream finishes the confection, making it a triple decker, cool sensation of a pie, hearkening back to the 1920s.

The signature crust for this pie is gingersnap, which can be made like a graham cracker crust using gingersnap cookie crumbs instead. You'll also find black bottom pies with chocolate wafer crusts, zwieback crusts, and standard graham cracker crusts, which is my favorite. This pie calls for a good long session of chilling in the refrigerator before you can cut and serve it. For the classic finishing flourish, grate some chocolate and sprinkle it on top of the whipped cream, right before you cut and serve this fabulous pie.

ONE 9-INCH GRAHAM CRACKER CRUST (STORE-BOUGHT OR SEE PAGE 146)

FILLING
1 TABLESPOON UNFLAVORED GELATIN

2 CUPS MILK

½ CUP SUGAR

4 TEASPOONS CORNSTARCH

¼ TEASPOON SALT

4 EGG YOLKS, BEATEN WELL

CHOCOLATE LAYER
2 SQUARES (2 OUNCES) UNSWEETENED CHOCOLATE

1 TEASPOON VANILLA EXTRACT

CUSTARD LAYER
4 EGG WHITES (TO SUBSTITUTE EGG WHITE POWDER, SEE NOTE)

¼ TEASPOON CREAM OF TARTAR

½ CUP SUGAR

1½ TEASPOONS ALMOND FLAVORING OR RUM FLAVORING

TOPPING
1 CUP HEAVY CREAM, VERY COLD

3 TABLESPOONS CONFECTIONERS' SUGAR

2 TABLESPOONS GRATED DARK CHOCOLATE (OPTIONAL)

Line a 9-inch pie pan with crust and then bake the crust as directed in the recipe.

To prepare the filling: In a small bowl, combine the gelatin and ¼ cup cold water. Stir well to dissolve the powder, and set aside. Scald the milk by warming it up in a heavy medium saucepan over medium heat, until small bubbles form around the edge of the pan, and steam rises off the milk; do not let it boil. Set aside.

In a medium bowl, whisk together the sugar, cornstarch, and salt. Add the egg yolks and stir to combine everything well. While stirring, carefully pour in about ¼ cup of the hot milk, and keep stirring to warm the yolks without cooking them into scrambled eggs. Add another ¼ cup of milk, stir well, and then stir the warmed egg yolk mixture into the saucepan of scalded milk.

(continued)

Place the pan over medium heat and cook, stirring almost constantly, until the mixture thickens, releases steam, and is thick enough to coat the back of a spoon, 5 to 10 minutes. Avoid letting the filling come to a boil, and stir well to keep it from sticking to the bottom of the pan. Remove from the heat, and stir the gelatin mixture into the filling, stirring well to dissolve it. Set aside.

To prepare the chocolate layer: Melt the chocolate in a small saucepan over medium-low heat, or in a medium heatproof bowl in a microwave. Scoop out half the warm filling mixture, and add it to the pan of melted chocolate, along with the vanilla. (Set the remaining custard aside for the second layer.) Stir the chocolate and custard together, mixing them evenly and well. Pour this mixture into the piecrust and spread it out into an even layer. Refrigerate the piecrust while you prepare the second layer of filling.

To prepare the custard layer: In a medium bowl, combine the egg whites and cream of tartar, and beat on medium speed until they are foamy and frothy, about 1 minute. Increase the speed to high, and when they turn white and begin to swell up, add the sugar gradually, beating all the while, until the egg whites are thick, white, shiny, and will hold firm peaks. Scoop the beaten egg whites into the remaining filling, and add the flavoring as well. Gently fold the egg whites into the custard, mixing evenly and well. Pour the custard over the chocolate filling in the crust, spreading and smoothing it to cover the chocolate completely and evenly. Cover the surface with plastic wrap to prevent a skin from forming and refrigerate the pie for 3 hours and as long as 1 day.

Shortly before serving, make the topping: Beat the cream in a medium bowl on high speed until it holds soft peaks. Add the sugar and continue beating just until it holds firm peaks. Quickly spread the whipped cream on the pie and use the back of a spoon to form pretty swirls. Sprinkle the grated chocolate on top if you like, and serve cold.

NOTE: This recipe not only demands more time and careful attention to detail, it also conspires to put many of your utensils to work at one time. To prepare, set out a heavy medium saucepan for the custard; a small saucepan for melting the chocolate (or a microwave-safe bowl); several mixing bowls, medium and large ones for the custard in all its incarnations and small ones for stirring sugar with cornstarch and gelatin with water, etc. You'll also need a whisk or big wooden spoons, measuring spoons, measuring cups, an electric mixer for whipping the cream, and spatulas for scraping bowls and pans. You'll have some dishes to wash, but that helps you pass time while the pie chills, and it is an extremely delicious pie. If possible, recruit a friend or family member to share the tasks (and pie!) with you.

To use powdered egg whites in the custard layer, measure out 3 tablespoons of egg white powder (see page 156) into a small bowl. Add ½ cup warm water, and stir well using a fork or a whisk to combine them evenly and well into a smooth, thick liquid. Stir for 2 to 3 minutes, so that the powder can absorb the liquid. Continue according to recipe directions for using egg whites.

Tar Heel Pie

MAKES ONE 9-INCH PIE

Being a North Carolina native with a lifelong affection for and dedication to my home state's traditional dishes, I can safely say that Tar Heel Pie is not an old, traditional recipe of the Tar Heel State. If I were a wagering kind of person, I would bet that it is of fairly recent nativity, probably since the 1980s. I would further presume that it might have arisen in response to a certain confection of rather similar provenance (Derby Pie) that is adored in the Bluegrass State of Kentucky, but that would be pure conjecture and it's really time to get back to this pie. Wherever it came from, I can declare with full authority that it is much loved here in North Carolina, and that it is one deliciously rich pie, which is dangerously easy to make. This is one where you should avoid having all the ingredients in the house, so as to prevent yourself from making unwise choices without proper forethought and consideration—the kind that triumphs when you contemplate having to go to the store. Best to enjoy this once in a great while, with whipped cream as an alluring option.

PASTRY FOR A 9-INCH SINGLE-CRUST PIE (STORE-BOUGHT OR SEE BASIC PIECRUSTS, PAGE 134)

½ CUP BUTTER

I CUP (6 OUNCES) SEMISWEET CHOCOLATE CHIPS

½ CUP ALL-PURPOSE FLOUR

½ CUP GRANULATED SUGAR

½ CUP PACKED LIGHT OR DARK BROWN SUGAR

I CUP (2 OUNCES) CHOPPED PECANS

2 EGGS, BEATEN WELL

I TEASPOON VANILLA EXTRACT

Heat the oven to 350 degrees F. Line a 9-inch pie pan with crust and then crimp the edges decoratively (see page 138).

In a small saucepan, melt the butter over medium-high heat, tilting and swirling the pan to melt it evenly. Remove it from the heat and add the chocolate chips. Stir quickly to melt the chocolate chips in the warm butter and to combine them well.

In a medium bowl, combine the flour and sugars and stir with a fork or a whisk to mix them well. Add the pecans and toss to coat them evenly with the flour mixture. Add the eggs, vanilla, and the chocolate mixture. Stir to mix everything together evenly into a thick, rich, nutty chocolate filling. Pour the filling into the piecrust.

Place the pie on the lowest shelf of the oven. Bake until the pie is puffy, handsomely browned, somewhat dry, and firm in the middle, 30 to 40 minutes.

Place the pie on a cooling rack or a folded kitchen towel and let cool to room temperature.

Peanut Butter–Banana Cream Pie with Fudge Sauce

MAKES ONE 9-INCH PIE AND ABOUT 3 CUPS FUDGE SAUCE

Born and raised in the Carolinas, Chefs Joe and Heidi Trull spent a decade cooking in New Orleans, where Heidi was chef-owner of Elizabeth, and Joe worked as pastry chef at Emeril Lagasse's Crescent City restaurant, Nola. Now they're cooking together at their highly regarded restaurant Grits and Groceries, located in a former country store at Saylor's Crossroads near Belton, South Carolina. They now have room for a great big garden, horses, a sunflower patch, and plenty of play spaces for their young son, Tom. Joe came up with this fabulous pie during his days at Nola, and it remains true to his menu motto of providing "real food, done real good." Plan ahead for this recipe, as you will need to bake the piecrust in advance, and then refrigerate the filled pie for at least two hours before serving.

PASTRY FOR A 9-INCH SINGLE-CRUST PIE (STORE-BOUGHT OR SEE BASIC PIECRUSTS, PAGE 134)

FILLING
12 OUNCES (1½ CUPS) CREAM CHEESE, SOFTENED
¾ CUP CONFECTIONERS' SUGAR
¾ CUP CREAMY PEANUT BUTTER

2 TABLESPOONS MILK
½ CUP (2 OUNCES) FINELY CHOPPED ROASTED PEANUTS, UNSALTED OR SALTED
3 CUPS HEAVY CREAM
3 BANANAS, SLICED ¼ INCH THICK
¼ CUP GRANULATED SUGAR

FUDGE SAUCE
1 CUP (6 OUNCES) FINELY CHOPPED UNSWEETENED CHOCOLATE
1 CUP HEAVY CREAM
⅔ CUP GRANULATED SUGAR
⅔ CUP PACKED LIGHT OR DARK BROWN SUGAR
⅓ CUP BUTTER

Line a 9-inch deep-dish pie pan with crust and then crimp the edges decoratively (see page 138). Line and fully bake the crust (see page 139). Set it aside to cool.

To make the filling: In a large bowl with an electric mixer, combine the cream cheese, confectioners' sugar, and peanut butter. Beat on medium speed until the mixture is light and fluffy. Add the milk and half of the peanuts, and beat to mix everything well.

In another large bowl, beat 2 cups of the cream until it thickens and holds firm peaks. Add the whipped cream to the peanut butter mixture and fold gently to combine them evenly into a smooth, thick filling. Add the sliced bananas, and then pour the filling into the baked piecrust. Smooth out the filling, mounding it up into a nice peak in the center of the pie. Cover and refrigerate for at least 2 hours before serving.

To make the fudge sauce: Place the chocolate in a medium heatproof bowl and set aside. In a medium saucepan, combine the cream, sugars, and butter over medium heat. Cook, stirring often, to melt the butter and dissolve the sugars into a smooth sauce. Pour the warm cream mixture over the chopped chocolate, stirring to melt the chocolate and combine everything into a smooth, thick fudge sauce. Set aside until serving time.

When ready to serve, combine the remaining 1 cup cream with the granulated sugar in a medium bowl. Beat on high speed until the cream holds firm peaks. Spread the whipped cream over the top of the pie, and sprinkle with the remaining peanuts. Serve cold, along with the fudge sauce.

BASIC PIECRUSTS

The phrase "easy as pie" still sits on the shelf of our everyday American language, but very few people outside of professional pie makers, culinary students, and trained pastry chefs would be likely to use it as a means to say, "This is easy and you can do it!" I wondered at it myself, even though I've learned how to make a good piecrust along the way. In researching this book of Southern pies, I've come to believe that we wonder at it because we focus on the wrong part of the process. When old-time cooks declared something to be "easy as pie," I think they meant, easy as molasses pie, or egg custard pie, or brown sugar pie—the minimalist pies of everyday baking. This was not only in the South, but all over the country in the days when home baking was neither hobby nor badge of accomplishment, but rather something that women in charge of feeding their families were routinely called upon to do. Making piecrust wasn't something to regard with pride, relief, or honor, but rather a task on her to-do list, in the realm of ironing, managing a checkbook, or canning tomatoes. Many women, generation after generation, up until the 1960s, got good at making piecrust the same way my grandmother got good at making biscuits: They had to do it, they learned the basics, they did it badly, and then not so well, and then decently, and then masterfully. By doing it again and again and again, moving through the process until their hands and eyes knew what to do, they got it down. I believe that "easy as pie" refers to the contents of the piecrust, not the dough itself, and in my particular interpretation, the phrase makes sense.

So many of the pie recipes in this book consist of stirring together a few basic ingredients, often the very same ones from pie type to pie type. Think chess pie, pecan pie, and sweet potato pie; or apple pie, peach pie, and the berry pies of summertime. With piecrust dough ready in the pan and a top crust ready to put in place, even these glorious fruit pies merely consist of cut-up fruit, simple sweetening and thickening, dots of butter, and a whisper of spices—and you're done. Press

(continued)

the top crust into place, cut a few steam vents, and into a hot oven it goes. The curtain falls, a little time passes, and presto—one fine, steaming, golden brown, irresistible pie. I'm being very optimistic here; some things can and do go wrong and not everybody will want to or be able to turn this around so easily, but I do believe that these homespun pies that have endured over time are completely master-able for almost any cook. Cakes have to rise, cool, come out of the pans in one piece, get stacked up, iced, and stay together despite gravity's longing to destabilize them. They may call for different fillings, or extra outside flourishes of coconut or nuts or glazes. But pie—you stir, you pour, you seal and vent, and you are likely to get a lovely tasty dessert.

All this leads me to the question of crust. It is the flag on the play, the flashing light in the rear-view mirror, the big orange sign that says, "Bridge out!" or "Detour," or even, "Abandon hope, all ye who enter here!" My advice is this: Take a low-key, "Why-not?," can-do attitude to pursue piecrust skill-building over the course of the next few months. Try some recipes in this chapter for starters. Ask for advice and demonstrations from friends or relatives who cook. Look for local cooking classes, or try to barter a great CD, a box of chocolates, or ripe sea-sonal fruit from the farmers' market in exchange for a lesson or two. Watch food television, and check out YouTube for culinary-oriented posts. Don't look for the ONE THING that is the trick, the secret, the moment of transformation. It's like life—you get in

there with a goal, and you go after it with spirit and joy. Most likely you will get what you set out to find, once you relax into the process and let it take its time.

Some of you will become makers of great pastry. Others will decide, "not for me!" Either way, as a cook—a person who can make a good piecrust from scratch—I am very, very glad to live and cook in a time when we can buy ready-to-bake piecrust dough as frozen shells, as refrigerated sheets, as dough to be rolled out, and as graham cracker crusts. Any of these routes are good ways to get you into action as a person who makes pies. I use ready-made piecrusts whenever I need the gift of time—when the goal is to get a given pie made up and into oven or fridge, ASAP. I also use the recipes here, and many others, when I want to make pie-crust dough from scratch. Here you will find five basic recipes: one for a butter crust (page 140), one for a butter and shortening crust (page 144), one for a lard crust (page 142), one for a canola oil crust (page 145), and one for a cookie crumb crust (page 146), which in this case is graham cracker crust. Each has its up-sides and down-sides, each could be made by hand or using a food processor, and each can be made in advance and refrigerated or frozen, covered tightly, until you are ready to make that pie. I hope that these piecrust recipes get you going on the road to homemade pies, whether you are an old hand or a first-time pie person. May you, in the process, one way or the other, end up reclaiming the phrase, "Easy as pie!"

Piecrust Particulars

GETTING A HEAD START ON PIECRUST

To make piecrust in advance, mix up the dough, roll it out, and even place it in a pie pan and crimp the edge of the crust by pinching it gently between your thumb and forefinger. Then you can wrap it well and refrigerate the piecrust for up to 3 days, or freeze it for up to 2 months. Once it is baked, you will need to use it within a day, and treat it very gently, as it crumbles easily. It's best to bake it as close to the time you will use it as possible.

MIXING IT UP

For making piecrust dough, cold is good because it helps keep the fat solid, which makes it form flaky layers when it bakes. You'll want super-cold fat, whether it's butter, shortening, or lard. Even frozen can be good if it's an especially hot day. I've had success with freezing fat and then grating it quickly on the large holes of a box grater. Some cooks even chill the bowl and flour, for extra "insurance."

ROLLING IT OUT

Cold piecrust dough is easier to roll out. Have a good supply of flour handy as you roll. Too much can make dough heavy, but for keeping it from sticking, dust the surface and the rolling pin lightly and often, and you'll find that flour is your friend. You can also roll the dough between layers of waxed paper.

STORE-BOUGHT PIECRUSTS

Nowadays, you can find piecrust dough in a wide array of forms. The refrigerator case in most supermarkets has round sheets of piecrust dough, all ready for fitting into a pie pan. In the freezer case, you'll find piecrusts fitted into aluminum foil pans, ready for filling and baking. Some stores also carry frozen circles of rolled-out piecrust dough, which you can keep in the freezer until about 30 minutes before you want to use them. Then remove, let them thaw, and fit them into the pie pan of your choice. Be sure that any kind of store-bought piecrust is kept wrapped up airtight, and either refrigerated or frozen until close to the time you will turn it into a pie.

MAKING A LATTICE TOP

Lattice tops make a simple, pretty alternative to a top crust for a double-crust pie or cobbler. To make a very simple lattice top, roll out one recipe of piecrust to make a 12-inch circle that is about ¼ inch thick. Slice the dough into long strips about ¾ inch wide. Arrange the pastry strips on top of the filling in a criss-cross pattern, weaving them into a lattice design, or simply laying the strips on top of each other. (Press any leftover pastry into a little disk, wrap well, and keep for your next pie; 1 week in the refrigerator or 2 months in the freezer.) Press the strips of pastry firmly up against the sides or edges of the bottom crust, dabbing on a little water if needed to seal them well. Fold the edges of the bottom crust up and over the rim, enclosing the sealed strips, and press down to seal the edge of the crust. Press the back of a table fork into the crust, working all the way around the pie to seal it completely.

BLIND BAKING (BAKING PIECRUST IN ADVANCE)

Some pies call for partially or fully baked piecrusts. These are often for pies that will not be baked at all or will not be baked for very long. To pre-bake a piecrust: Heat the oven to 375 degrees F. Line the empty piecrust with parchment paper or waxed paper (this is called "blind baking"). Then fill it with dried beans or rice, to keep the dough from shrinking and the sides from collapsing as it cooks. Bake until the crust is very lightly browned and somewhat dry, about 10 minutes. For a partially baked (par-baked) piecrust, stop at this point and proceed according to the recipe directions for filling and baking the pie. For a fully baked piecrust, remove the pie pan from the oven, and carefully lift out the parchment paper and rice or beans. Return the now-exposed piecrust to the oven until it is dry and nicely and evenly browned, 10 to 12 minutes. Remove, cool, and proceed with recipe.

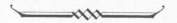

Butter Piecrust

MAKES TWO 9-INCH SINGLE PIECRUSTS OR ONE 9-INCH DOUBLE PIECRUST

My friend and fellow food writer Sandra Gutierrez generously shared her butter piecrust recipe, which provides butter's delicious flavor and a rich texture. As with any piecrust, the colder your ingredients, the more delicate and pleasing your pastry is likely to be. This recipe is made in a food processor; you could also use a pastry blender or two table knives to cut the butter and shortening into the flour.

2 CUPS ALL-PURPOSE FLOUR

I TEASPOON SALT

½ CUP VERY COLD UNSALTED BUTTER, CUT INTO ½-INCH CUBES

4 TO 6 TABLESPOONS ICE WATER

I TEASPOON WHITE VINEGAR

In the workbowl of a food processor fitted with a metal blade, combine the flour and salt; pulse for 10 seconds. Add the butter cubes and pulse until the mixture resembles coarse sand with some small lumps, 30 to 40 seconds.

Add 3 tablespoons of the ice water and the vinegar and pulse 5 to 7 times, until the dough just barely holds together in the workbowl. Add another tablespoon or two of ice water if needed just to bring the ingredients together. Turn it out onto plastic wrap and pat the dough into two separate disks; refrigerate them for at least 1 hour. Set one or two disks out at room temperature for 10 minutes before rolling.

Roll out one of the dough disks on a lightly floured surface, to a circle about ⅛ inch thick and 10 inches wide. Carefully transfer it into a 9-inch pie plate. Press the dough gently into the pan and trim away any excess dough, leaving about ½ inch beyond the edge of the pie pan. Fold the edges up and over, and then crimp the edges decoratively. Or press the back of a fork into the pastry rim, working around the pie to make a flat edge marked with the tines of the fork. If not filling the crust soon, refrigerate it until needed.

To make the crust in advance, wrap it well in plastic and refrigerate it for up to 3 days, or freeze it for up to 2 months.

"You Can Do This" Lard Piecrust

MAKES ONE 9-INCH SINGLE PIECRUST

My friend Robin Kline, a brilliant cook, had mastered just about every culinary challenge except that of making piecrust. Perhaps because she is Southern, with a Southern pastry-making Mama, she felt compelled to give it One More Try. Unfolding her mother's carefully written recipe, she got busy and got it right. Not only did she succeed, she now stirs up and rolls out twelve to fifteen sheets of piecrust in one session, so that she can bake up big batches of homemade pies for her local shelter.

This recipe calls for a kitchen scale, a mixing bowl that can be used to weigh out ingredients, and a pastry blender (see page 9). Many chefs and cooks prefer measuring by weight, instead of by volume, since it allows for maximum consistency and precision in terms of ingredient amounts and allows for simple, speedy measurement of dry ingredient amounts when baking in quantity. I've included volume measurements as well so that you can make this piecrust without a scale.

3 OUNCES (ABOUT ¼ CUP) LARD

5½ OUNCES (1½ CUPS) ALL-PURPOSE FLOUR

½ TEASPOON SALT

4 TO 6 TABLESPOONS ICE WATER

Place a large bowl on a kitchen scale, and weigh the lard. Add just enough flour to the bowl to make a total weight of 8½ ounces, sprinkling the flour over the lard as you weigh it out. Remove the bowl from the scale, and add the salt.

Using a pastry blender, cut the lard into the flour until well blended and you have small pea-sized pieces of lard in the flour. Very quickly sprinkle about 3 tablespoons of the ice water over the flour-lard mixture, stirring quickly and gently with a fork, to bring everything together into a crumbly mass of dough. Add another tablespoon or two of ice water if needed just to bring the ingredients together.

Scoop up the dough in the palms of your hand, and press it together into a flat disk about 4 inches across. Wrap the dough disk in plastic wrap or waxed paper, and refrigerate it for 1 hour, until cold. Set the dough out at room temperature for 10 minutes before rolling.

Scatter flour onto a countertop, and use a rolling pin to roll out the piecrust into a 10-inch circle. Use long, quick, short strokes, moving quickly to roll out the crust. Carefully transfer it into a 9-inch pie plate. Press the dough gently into the pan and trim away any excess dough, leaving about ½ inch beyond the edge of the pie pan. Fold the edges up and over, and then crimp the edges decoratively. Or press the back of a fork into the pastry rim, working around the pie to make a flat edge marked with the tines of the fork. If not filling the crust soon, refrigerate it until needed, up to 3 days.

NOTE: You can freeze this dough, shaped into a disk and well wrapped, for up to 3 weeks. Let the frozen dough thaw in the refrigerator for several hours before rolling it out. You could also roll it out, place it in a pie pan, shape the crust for a single-crust pie, wrap well, and then freeze the oven-ready piecrust for up to 3 weeks.

ROBIN'S PASTRY-MAKING TIPS

"I use a wire pastry blender, only touching the pastry with my hands to quickly shape it into a ball. I press it into a flat disk about 4 inches across, wrap in plastic wrap and chill for an hour. This hour's time gives me a chance to clean up, prepare my pie filling, and read the paper with a cup of coffee."

"I use a rolling pin with ball bearings for a wicked spin, which helps in making the quick, short strokes I recommend for a fairly evenly round crust."

Butter/Shortening Piecrust

MAKES TWO 9-INCH SINGLE PIECRUSTS

This recipe comes from Chef Barry Maiden, of Hungry Mother Restaurant in Cambridge, Massachusetts. It's wonderful with any pie filling, but do try it with his scrumptious Hungry Mother Spicy Peanut Pie (page 56). His piecrust uses a combination of butter and shortening. The butter delivers flavor, while shortening provides a flaky texture. The soft texture of this dough makes it best for single-crust pies.

1½ CUPS ALL-PURPOSE FLOUR

2 TABLESPOONS SUGAR

½ TEASPOON SALT

10 TABLESPOONS (⅔ CUP) VERY COLD UNSALTED BUTTER, CUT INTO ½-INCH CUBES

2 TABLESPOONS VERY COLD VEGETABLE SHORTENING

3 TABLESPOONS ICE WATER

Put the flour, sugar, and salt in a bowl and put them in the freezer for 10 minutes.

Put the flour, sugar, salt, butter, and shortening in the workbowl of a food processor fitted with a metal blade. Pulse to cut the fat into small pieces, some the size of peas and some smaller.

With the machine running, slowly pour the water through the feed tube. The dough should begin to come together into a ball; when it does, turn off the machine immediately. Do not let it form a complete ball.

Turn the dough out onto a floured work surface and gently shape it into two disks about 1½ inches thick. Wrap the disks in plastic wrap and refrigerate them for 30 minutes to 1 hour.

Take the dough out of the refrigerator and let it sit for 10 minutes. On a floured surface, roll out one of the dough disks into a circle ¼ inch thick and 10 inches wide. Carefully transfer it into a 9-inch pie plate. Press the dough gently into the pan and trim away any excess dough, leaving about ½ inch beyond the edge of the pie pan. Fold the edges up and over, and then crimp the edges decoratively. Or press the back of a fork into the pastry rim, working around the pie to make a flat edge marked with the tines of the fork. If not filling the crust soon, refrigerate it until needed.

To make the crust in advance, wrap it well in plastic and refrigerate it for up to 3 days or freeze it for up to 2 months.

Canola Oil Piecrust

This crust is the one to turn to when rolling out piecrust dough presents a problem. Whether you're without the requisite rolling pin, or simply not a confident piecrust maker, this crust provides you a simple solution: It's a soft dough that you press into the pie plate by hand, as you would do with a graham cracker crumb crust.

1 ½ CUPS ALL-PURPOSE FLOUR	½ TEASPOON SALT	2 TABLESPOONS COLD MILK
1 ½ TEASPOONS SUGAR	½ CUP CANOLA OIL	

In a medium bowl, combine the flour, sugar, and salt. Use a fork or a whisk to stir them together well.

In a small bowl, combine the oil and milk. Use a fork to mix them together into a frothy mixture. (Or put them in a jar with a lid and shake well to combine them.)

Scoop out a well in the flour mixture. Pour the oil-milk mixture into the flour, and use a fork to bring the liquid and dry ingredients together into a crumbly mixture.

Divide the dough in half. Carefully pat one half of the dough into a 9-inch pie plate, distributing it evenly. Use your hands to build up the sides, covering the pan well and pinching the rim to make a small edge around the top of the piecrust. Repeat with the remaining dough to make a second crust.

Wrap and refrigerate the crusts for up to 2 days or freeze for up to 3 weeks.

Graham Cracker Crust

Graham cracker crumb crusts provide a delicious and appealing foundation for many kinds of pie, and are easy for any type of cook to make. Crumb crusts are particularly popular with pies that are served cold, such as Key Lime Pie (page 106), chiffon pies, ice cream pies, and pies with a delicate cheesecake-type filing. You can prepare several ahead of time and keep them frozen for up to one month. You can make crumb crusts with almost any crisp cookie, such as gingersnaps, chocolate wafers, and vanilla wafers. Bake the crust if you can, for the sturdiest texture. If you can't bake it, chill it for two hours before filling it, and for several hours or overnight before cutting and serving the pie.

1¼ CUPS GRAHAM CRACKER CRUMBS
(ABOUT 15 SQUARES; SEE NOTE)

3 TABLESPOONS SUGAR

⅓ CUP BUTTER, MELTED

Heat the oven to 350 degrees F.

In a medium bowl, combine the graham cracker crumbs and sugar and stir with a fork to mix them well. Add the butter and stir to mix it into the crumbs evenly and well.

Press the buttery crumbs into a 9-inch pie pan, distributing the mixture evenly, and pressing firmly with your hands or another pie pan of the same size, to flatten the crumbs and shape a sturdy crust to hold the filling. Make sure to work the crumbs up to the rim of the pan, to make an good, strong edge.

Place the crust on the center shelf of the oven. Bake until the crust is heated through and lightly browned, 8 to 10 minutes.

Place the crust on a cooling rack or a folded kitchen towel and let cool to room temperature before adding the filling.

NOTE: To make crumbs by hand, break the graham crackers into small pieces, crumbling them over a medium bowl. Put the pieces in the bottom of a large plastic bag. Using a rolling pin or large full can of soup or evaporated milk, crush the cracker pieces into a fine powder, rolling and smashing gently, to crumble up the cracker pieces without breaking open the bag. Measure out 1 ¼ cups, and prepare the crust as described. To make crumbs using a food processor, break the graham crackers into medium pieces, and put them into the workbowl of a food processor that has been fitted with the metal blade. Pulse to break the pieces down into bits, and then process until you have fine crumbs, stopping once or twice to scrape the sides and grind them evenly.

Glossary for Southern Pies

ALMONDS

Almonds are anything but absent from the American table, but their place in the Southern cook's larder has shrunk greatly from where it was in colonial days. Southern recipes calling for ground or crushed almonds and almond paste were everywhere in early American cookbooks; see Almond Custard Pie (page 30) for an example of an old-time dessert that works wonderfully today. Peanuts and pecans became local favorites, since they are grown in the South, and perhaps their mere presence as less-expensive nuts put almonds on the back burner in terms of the pantry and the oven. California is now the main source for almonds, but in the seventeenth and eighteenth centuries, almonds most likely came from Spain. The basic *frangipane*, a custard of ground almonds, sugar, and eggs, remains popular in European kitchens, and belongs in any home baker's basic repertoire.

ALMOND PASTE

Blanched and ground into a fine, substantial paste that is almost a sticky dough, almond paste forms the basis for Almond Custard Pie (page 30). It is available in the baking section of supermarkets, and from baking ingredient mail-order sources (see page 156). To make your own, use a food processor; use a sturdy mortar and pestle if you want a traditional kitchen version using the handheld "food processor" of old.

APPLES

The book *Old Southern Apples* (now out of print) by Creighton Lee Calhoun (page 158), is a masterpiece and a must for anyone interested in the subject of old Southern apple varieties. Whether you want to know about them or to grow them, you need this book.

BLACK WALNUTS

Black walnut trees still grow wild throughout the South, particularly in West Virginia, Kentucky, and the Appalachian mountain range. They are an accessible luxury in mountain cooking, and a joy to country cooks and old-timers everywhere you travel in the South. Beloved for their rich, memorable, and peculiar flavor, they are a big mess to work with (purple stains all over your hands and clothes), and extremely difficult to crack. Wonderful in cakes, pound cakes, fudge, and pies (page 108), though, they are worth a lot of trouble. Seek them out in farmers' markets during the fall; check with the produce manager at your local supermarket, or order a supply for your winter baking (see page 156).

BLACKBERRIES

This once-a-year treat is a treasure in the wild for the Southern kitchen and table. Thorny blackberry canes spring up and thrive year after year down in the ditches, along the edges of fields, up the hillsides, and in areas that are widely considered "snakey" and that harbor the dreaded "chiggers"—a tenacious little insect that pounces on blackberry pickers and delivers days of powerful and maddening itching. "Why bother?" one might ask, but only if one had never had my grandmother's blackberry rolls or her jam or her preserves. (I missed the wine due to being an underage grandchild during her wine-making era.) They are divine in preserves, jams, jellies, pies, cobblers, dumplings, and just eaten out of hand. See Karen Wilcher's Old-Time Blackberry Cobbler (page 73) for a wonderful recipe. Nowadays you'll find you-pick-'em sites with thornless domesticated varieties that are also lovely and delicious. Look for those, check farmers' markets, and also plant some blackberry bushes in your backyard, keeping in mind that they do like to spread!

BLACKSTRAP MOLASSES

See "molasses"

BUTTERMILK

Excellent in baking, buttermilk gives tenderness and tang. It has been used widely in baking wherever dairy products were available, and that means if you had and milked your own cow or cows. During times when people churned fresh milk into butter, buttermilk was a natural leftover that found its use. Nowadays it's made from a commercial culture, like yogurt, and widely available in supermarkets. Look for buttermilk from specialty/artisan dairies for the absolute best, old-time flavor. You can also use dried buttermilk powder, which is stirred into the dry ingredients. For a decent substitute, stir 1 tablespoon of vinegar or lemon juice into 1 cup of milk, and let it stand for 10 to 20 minutes to develop a tangy flavor and thickened texture.

CHOCOLATE

Chocolate figures in American cooking from colonial times forward, but for reasons that are unfathomable to me, it found little favor in the world of pies until the turn of the twentieth century. Ice cream? Sure thing. Candy? You bet! Puddings, icings, and eventually cake batters? Of course! But pies with chocolate in them took a while. The earliest chocolate used was unsweetened, grated from substantial blocks and chunks. The turn of the twentieth century saw cocoa powder's rise to popularity, particularly for Southern cooks and bakers.

COBBLER

Cobbler doesn't fit into a description box, the way that cakes and pies do. Regional variations abound, even within the South. The classic Southern cobbler usually involves fruit enclosed in a pastry crust, but then there's also sweet potato cobbler. Top and bottom crusts are standard, forming a kind of deep-dish pie baked in a square or rectangular pan. Biscuit-topped cobblers are another traditional Southern dessert. A modern version of cobbler involves a cake batter poured over sweetened fruit or poured into a pan with fruit added over it. For this book, I've focused on the pielike incarnation of cobbler like the one featured (page 73), with a full pastry or lattice top. The idea for cobblers may have come from a need for quantity. You had an abundance of fruit from the blackberry canes, the sour cherry trees, or the trip home from the beach where you picked up bushels of peaches. There were lots of people to feed, so you made big pans of cobbler, which is easily scooped out into small serving bowls, rather than portioned out into wedges like a pie. The ubiquitous sweet finish of North Carolina barbecue places, a pastry-covered fruit cobbler is easily made up and dished out for a busy-day dessert.

DAMSON PLUMS

These are wild, small, deep purple plums beloved in old Southern culinary circles. "Damson" references their origin in the ancient Syrian city of Damascus. Brought to England by the Romans, and then by English colonists to America early in the colonial era, damson plum trees took to their new home and have been thriving here for several hundred years. With their small size and very tart skin, they shine in such culinary applications as the making of jams, jellies, wine, and pies, rather than for eating out of hand. This hardy fruit with a deep rich flavor and gorgeous color was valued for making clothing dyes as well. Read Edna Lewis on the subject in *The Taste of Country Cooking*, and look for artisan-made damson plum jams and jellies at farmers' markets. Then you can make the lovely Damson Plum Custard Pie (page 25).

DRIED APPLES

It was a standard practice throughout the rural South to dry apples, anywhere that apple trees would grow. You simply slice them thinly (peeled and cored), then dry them in the sun for days until they are soft and pliant but no longer moist. Dried apples were often stored for winter baking and eating, stewed into an applesauce, cooked to jammy lusciousness with sugar, and tucked into pies. Spices such as cinnamon, nutmeg, mace, and allspice were common counterparts but not always employed; many mountain cooks preferred to let pure, simple apple flavor reign supreme.

EVAPORATED MILK

Developed in the 1880s, but not widely used until the early twentieth century, evaporated milk quickly became a staple of Southern kitchens. Fresh milk was a luxury for many until refrigeration became common, and the Pet Milk Company, which worked out the kinks in safe production of this form of milk and marketed it widely in the 1930s, became the household name for this product for several generations of Southern cooks.

KEY LIMES

Key limes are a tiny, yellow-green citrus with thin skins. Key lime pie is the signature dish of the Key Islands, forming a necklace of paradise destinations off the south coast of Florida. While their flavor is distinctive, a supply of fresh Key limes has always been a luxury for Southern cooks. If you can't find fresh ones, you can substitute an equal amount of lime juice from the big, round, dark green Persian limes that are easy to find year-round.

MOLASSES

A by-product of the process of refining sugar, molasses is dark, rustic, and robustly sweet. It lends its handsome color to food along with its earthy flavor, and its texture ranges between that of honey and maple syrup. When the weather turns cold, it all but sets up and needs scooping instead of pouring. You can use unsulphured molasses interchangeably with ordinary molasses, which won't actually be labeled "sulphured." Pure cane syrup is its more delicately flavored and lighter-in-texture first cousin, made from an earlier step in sugar processing, and blackstrap molasses is made from the final processing. Though molasses is nutritious, the concentrated flavor of blackstrap makes it less than ideal as a substitute for molasses in cooking sweet dishes. You can interchange pure cane syrup, sorghum, honey, molasses, and maple syrup in recipes with good, though not identical, results. Corn syrups can also be substituted, but their flavor is so mild that you will lose any layer of rustic depth, getting mostly thick texture and one-note sweetness.

OLEO

Oleo is an abbreviation for the term "oleomargarine," since shortened to "margarine" somewhere along the way. Home-style cookbooks from the first half of the twentieth century often refer to *oleo*. I substitute an equal amount of butter in those recipes.

ORANGE FLOWER WATER

Also called "orange blossom water," this aromatic and flavorful essence distilled from the blossoms of bitter orange was much prized in the colonial kitchen. Of Middle Eastern origin, its perfume and taste enhanced baked goods, including pound cakes, scones, and tea cakes. See the "Rose Water" entry on the following page for more details. Check Middle Eastern markets or mail order (see page 156) for sources.

PECANS

A native nut, pecan trees have been domesticated for generations, and they thrive all over the South. The backyard pecan tree was common a hundred years ago, and gathering, cracking, and picking out these delicious sweet nuts is an autumn ritual still worthy of making your own. The pecan-gathering expedition and cooking session in Truman Capote's story "A Christmas Memory" is the perfect read-aloud for a pecan-cracking session by the fire or kitchen table. Whole, chopped, or finely ground, pecans are Southern culinary gold.

PERSIMMONS

Wild persimmon trees still pepper the Southern countryside, undulating out of wooded groves on the edge of many a farmstead's plowed fields. Look up around the time of the first frost, and you may be lucky enough to find a spindly tree laden with what might be tiny Christmas ornaments, tempting both the bird population and the traditional cook to come and get an edible treasure that is the epitome of fall in color, texture, and plush-yet-tangy flavor. Most often made into a baked pudding served in squares, persimmons make a deliciously dense, glistening, orange-colored pie (see page 94), which is even better the second day.

Hachiya and Fuyu, two widely available domesticated varieties of persimmons, will work nicely in any persimmon recipe. Ranging in size between a small apple and a large pear, both are easier to prepare than their wild cousins, due to their larger size and the fact that they have fewer seeds. Processing fresh, ripe, wild persimmons is and has always been a pursuit for the dedicated cook, as they are a glorious mess—imbued with a vivid, staining color. They are also studded with an unbelievable number of sturdy brown seeds; so many that a food mill surrenders and calls in a sieve as reinforcement. To prepare wild persimmons, place about twenty-four whole, unpeeled persimmons in a large sieve, and press them through, working tenaciously, using a large flat spoon and your hands. Scrape pulp from the outside of the sieve, discard the seeds, and continue in this way.

To use Fuyu or Hachiya persimmons, remove the core first. For firm, solid fruit, peel away the skin using a vegetable peeler or paring knife. If they are soft and mushy, halve each one lengthwise and scoop and squeeze out the persimmon pulp, discarding the soft skin. Chop firm persimmons into two-inch chunks. Purée the persimmon pulp in a blender or food processor until smooth and thick. If the purée is stringy and uneven in texture, you can press it through a sieve. Persimmon purée freezes very well, so if you can gather a supply in the fall, prepare it, freeze it in one-cup portions, and enjoy through the year.

PLUMS
See "Damson Plums"

ROSE WATER
This flavoring, a lovely and delicious essence distilled from rose petals, was a standard favorite in English cooking long before colonial American kitchens got fired up for baking. It came to Europe via trade and conquerors in the Middle East. Along with orange flower water (page 152), it was much enjoyed in early American cuisine, particularly in sweets from pound cakes and marzipan to jumbles, macaroons, and a delicate pudding called "flummery." Rose water fell from use along the way as vanilla and almond extracts rose to be queens of the essence and flavoring category. Look for it today in Middle Eastern markets, or see page 156.

We've come to associate its aroma with perfumes and fragrant soaps, but if you get past that startling sensation, you may find that you appreciate its delicate notes, as I do. It won't be sending vanilla and almond extracts packing, but it's a lovely antique that would be welcome on the specialty shelf to my mind.

SONKER
This is the regional name for an oversized deep-dish cobbler, made for as long as anyone can remember in Surry County, North Carolina. A large pan is completely lined with pastry, filled with fruit, enhanced with sugar, butter, and spices, then baked and served with a sauce known as "dip." Served on the side for pouring over individual servings, dip is most commonly a sweet milk sauce thickened with cornstarch, but a custard version with egg and butter is also widely enjoyed. See page 101.

SORGHUM

Sorghum is a tall, long-leaved grass grown in the South and particularly in the mountain regions, to be harvested in fall and ground into a juice that is cooked down into a delicious and nutritious syrup. People used to grind their own sorghum at home or take it to a small local sorghum mill, often paying with a portion of their crop's syrup. Thinner than molasses or honey, sorghum has a deep, rich, molasses-like flavor, with a texture like maple syrup. Dark like black coffee, it is closest to pure cane syrup, but each is distinctive and worthy on its own account. The taste of sorghum is more delicate. A Southern mountain recipe from the nineteenth century calling for molasses probably referred to sorghum, since that is what people grew locally and easily and could therefore afford to have in a pitcher on the table, morning, noon, and night. With some butter, sorghum makes biscuits or cornbread into an indescribably delicious treat.

SWEET DOUGH

Sweet dough is the term for pastry made for pies, tarts, and handheld pies in Cajun South Louisiana. The dough has eggs, sugar, and leavening, and is soft, so that it is pressed more than rolled out. The classic use is tarte à la bouillie (page 112).

SWEET MILK

Known today just as "milk," this food item got the "sweet" designation to contrast it with "sour milk" and "buttermilk." Both of those first cousins in the milk family have exceptional value in cooking and baking, and were an essential part of Southern culinary life back in the days of milking the cow or listening for the milkman at the backdoor. For the most part, buttermilk and sour milk have become footnotes to kitchen history. Today's milk designations focus on exactly how many iotas of fat a given carton of the dairy product might contain. Sweet milk was the good stuff—precious and useful for drinking, and less valuable than buttermilk and sour milk in the eyes of a traditional Southern cook.

SWEET POTATOES

These trusty products of Southern soil are reliably grown, stored, and easily cooked in a variety of ways, making them a feature of feasts and simple suppers. Big, rounded, and a brashly beautiful orange inside, sweet potatoes are often called "yams'" by Southern cooks and eaters. They aren't the same vegetable, but down here, we really don't care about that too much. We often call them by their true name, sweet potatoes, but the dish "candied yams" just wouldn't have its aural magic if we had to properly identify its essential ingredient. Sweet potatoes were often roasted in the fireplace coals and carried to the fields in a lunch pail, mashed up with butter and spices and sugar, or sliced and candied with sugar and butter for a fine dinner side dish. They were also stirred into biscuit dough or pound cake batter, and most wonderfully, consistently baked into one of the South's finest pies (see page 34). The fried pie category also includes sweet potato–filled versions, which should be bought and consumed at every opportunity, so that they will live on in our food world. Sweet potatoes are a classic ingredient for North Carolina's signature "sonker" (see Sonkers, page 153). The tiny marshmallow "brûlée" finish for many of today's special-occasion meals in the South is a relatively recent addition to the sweet potato pantheon; I see this as evolution in our affection for the sweet potato, evidence that home cooks want to keep on coming up with reasons for and ways of enjoying them.

SWEETENED CONDENSED MILK

Developed in the 1850s as a means to have a shelf-stable form of milk, sweetened condensed milk is still popular for its plush texture and sweetness in modern cooking and baking, especially in pies such as Key Lime Pie (page 106). It gave easy access to milk as both a beverage and an ingredient, long before refrigeration and easy transportation made it irrelevant to the cook whether you had a cow or not.

Sources for Southern Food and Cooking

The Baker's Catalog
King Arthur Flour
58 Billings Farm Road
White River Junction, VT 05001
(800) 827-6836
www.bakerscatalog.com
Equipment from rolling pins and pie pans to crust shields and nested stainless-steel bowls; ingredients from pastry flour to flavorings.

Geechee Sweets
P.O. Box 34
Sapelo Island, GA 31327
(912) 485-2262; (919) 485-2206
www.geecheesweets.com
Jams and jellies, including scuppernong and Muscadine grape jelly; books by Mrs. Cornelia Walker Bailey, keeping the traditions and history of Geechee and Gullah people and culture alive in the Sea Islands off the Georgia coast.

Hammons Products Company
105 Hammons Drive
P.O. Box 140
Stockton, MO 65785
www.black-walnuts.com
Black walnuts for baking, as well as nutcrackers (should you have a supply of black walnuts in need of cracking).

Hoppin' John's
(800) 828-4412
www.hoppinjohns.com
Cornmeal and grits: artisan made, stone ground, and of the highest quality; essential cookbooks by culinary historian and Southern food authority John Martin Taylor.

"Just Whites" Egg White Powder
Deb-El Foods Corporation
2 Papetti Plaza
Elizabeth, NJ 07206

Kalustyan's
123 Lexington Avenue
New York, NY 10016
(800) 352-3451; (212) 685-3451
www.kalustyans.com
Flavorings including Middle Eastern rose water and orange flower water; oil of bitter almonds; almond paste; pistachios.

The Lee Bros. Boiled Peanuts Catalog
P.O. Box 315
Charleston, SC 29402
(843) 720-8890
www.boiledpeanuts.com
Southern products galore, from black walnuts, cane syrup, jams, and jellies to sorghum and more.

Muddy Pond Sorghum Mill
4363 Muddy Pond Road
Monterey TN 38574
(931) 445-3589
www.muddypondsorghum.com
Wonderful sorghum from a Tennessee family farm.

Nellie & Joe's Famous Key Lime Juice
Key West, Florida
(800) LIME-PIE
www.keylimejuice.com
Bottled Key lime juice.

The Pampered Chef
(888) 687-2433
www.pamperedchef.com
Pie pans, rolling pins, pastry blenders, crust shields, etc.

Penzeys Spices
Brookfield, WI 53045
(800) 741-7787
www.penzeys.com
Excellent source for spices; seasonings; and flavoring extracts, including vanilla, almond, orange, and lemon.

SACO Foods
(800) 373-7226
www.sacofoods.com
Cultured buttermilk powder.

Southern Foodways Alliance
Center for the Study of Southern Culture
Barnard Observatory
P. O. Box 1848
University, MS 38677
(662) 915-5993
sfamail@olemiss.edu
www.southernfoodways.com
An organization dedicated to tracking down, celebrating, and preserving Southern culinary traditions and history and the people and stories behind them.

Steen's Pure Cane Syrup
P.O. Box 339
119 N. Main Street,
Abbeville, LA 70510
(800) 725-1654
www.steensyrup.com
Pure cane syrup and molasses.

Sur la Table
P.O. Box 34707
Seattle, WA 98124
(800) 243-0852
www.surlatable.com
Equipment including double boilers, wire cooling racks, pie pans, rolling pins, nested mixing bowl sets, cooking thermometers, measuring cups and spoons, sifters, kitchen parchment, cookbooks, etc.

Tucker Pecan Company
350 North McDonough Street
Montgomery, AL 36104
(800) 239-6540
www.tuckerpecan.com
Pecans and pecan candy and gift baskets.

Wholesome Sweeteners
8016 Highway 90-A
Sugar Land, TX 77478
(800) 680-1896
www.wholesomesweeteners.com
Fair trade, organic, delicious, and extensive in its range of products, all of them worthy and good for the world as well as good to your palate. Fair trade and organic brown sugar and white sugar, honey, agave, sugar, corn syrup, Sucanet; if you want sweet, start here.

Bibliography

Anderson, Jean. *A Love Affair with Southern Cooking*. New York: William Morrow, 2007.

———. *The American Century Cookbook: The Most Popular Recipes of the 20ᵗʰ Century*. New York: Clarkson Potter, 1997.

Barker, Karen. *Sweet Stuff*. Chapel Hill: The University of North Carolina Press, 2004.

Bienvenu, Marcelle. *Who's Your Mama, Are You Catholic, and Can You Make a Roux?* Lafayette, LA: Acadian House Publishing, 2006.

———, and Judy Walker. *Cooking Up a Storm: Recipes Lost and Found from The Times-Picayune of New Orleans*. San Francisco: Chronicle Books, 2008.

Brown, Marion. *The Southern Cook Book*. Chapel Hill: The University of North Carolina Press, 1951.

Calhoun, Creighton Lee. *Old Southern Apples*. Blacksburg, VA: The McDonald & Woodward Publishing Company, 1995.

Chase, Leah. *And Still I Cook*. Gretna, LA: Pelican Publishing Company, 2003.

———. *The Dooky Chase Cookbook*. Gretna, LA: Pelican Publishing Company, 2000.

Claiborne, Craig. *Craig Claiborne's Southern Cooking*. New York: Times Books/Random House, 1987.

Corriher, Shirley. *Bakewise: Secrets of Baking Revealed*. New York: Scribner, 2008.

Council, Mildred. *Mama Dip's Kitchen*. Chapel Hill: University of North Carolina Press, 2005.

———. *Mama Dip's Family Cookbook*. Chapel Hill: University of North Carolina Press, 2005.

Crawford, Willie. *Soul Food Recipes, Learned on a North Carolina Tobacco Farm*. Valparaiso, FL: WillieCrawford.com, 2001.

Dabney, Joseph E. *Smokehouse Ham, Spoon Bread, and Scuppernong Wine: The Folklore and Art of Southern Appalachian Cooking*. Nashville: Cumberland House, 1998.

Darden, Norma Jean, and Carole Darden. *Spoonbread and Strawberry Wine: Recipes and Reminiscences of a Family*. New York: Doubleday, 1994.

Dixon, Ethel. *Big Mama's Old Black Pot Recipes*. Alexandria, LA: Stoke Gabriel, 1987.

Dull, Henrietta Stanley. *Southern Cooking*. Atlanta: Ruralist Press, 1928. Reprinted by Cherokee Press, 1989.

Dupree, Nathalie. *Nathalie Dupree's Southern Memories: Recipes and Reminiscences*. New York: Clarkson Potter, 1993.

———. *New Southern Cooking*. New York: Alfred A. Knopf, 2004.

Edge, John T., ed. *A Gracious Plenty: Recipes and Recollections from the American South*. New York: G.P. Putnam's Sons, 1999.

———. *Southern Belly: The Food Lover's Companion to the South*. Chapel Hill: Algonquin Books, 2007.

Egerton, John. *Side Orders: Small Servings of Southern Food and Culture*. Atlanta: Peachtree Publishers, 1990.

————. *Southern Food*. New York: Alfred A. Knopf, 1987.

Estes, Rufus. *Rufus Estes' Good Things to Eat: The First Cookbook by an African-American Chef*. Reprint, Mineola, New York: Dover Publications, 2004.

Ferguson, Sheila. *Soul Food: Classic Cuisine from the Deep South*. New York: Weidenfeld and Nicholson, 1989.

Ferris, Marcie Cohen. *Matzoh Ball Gumbo: Culinary Tales of the Jewish South*. Chapel Hill: The University of North Carolina Press, 2005.

Fisher, Abby. *What Mrs. Fisher Knows about Old Southern Cooking: Soup, Pickles, Preserves, Etc*. San Francisco: Women's Cooperative Printing Office, 1881. Facsimile Edition. Reprint, Bedford, MA: Applewood Books, 1995.

Flagg, Fannie. *Fannie Flagg's Original Whistle Stop Café Cookbook*. New York: Gallantine, 1993.

Foose, Martha Hall. *Screen Doors and Sweet Tea: Recipes and Tales from a Southern Cook*. New York: Clarkson Potter, 2008.

Fowler, Damon Lee. *Classical Southern Cooking: A Celebration of the Cuisine of the Old South*. New York: Crown Publishing, 1995.

Fox, Minnie C. *The Blue Grass Cook Book*. Lexington, KY: University of Kentucky Press, 2005.

Grosvenor, Verta Mae. *Vibration Cooking: The Travel Notes of a Geechee Girl*. New York: Doubleday, 1970.

Guas, David. *DamGoodSweet*. Boston: Taunton Press, 2009.

Harris, Dr. Jessica B. *Beyond Gumbo: Creole Fusion Food from the Atlantic Rim*. New York: Simon & Schuster, 2003.

————. *The Welcome Table: African-American Heritage Cooking*. New York: Simon & Schuster, 1995.

Hess, Karen. *The Carolina Rice Kitchen*. Columbia, SC: University of South Carolina Press, 1992.

Joachim, David, and Andrew Schloss. *The Science of Good Food*. Toronto, Ontario, Canada: Robert Rose, Inc., 2008.

Jones, Wilbert. *Mama's Tea Cakes: 101 Delicious Soul Food Desserts*. New York: Birch Lane Press/Kensington, 1998.

Lee, Matt, and Ted Lee. *The Lee Brothers' Southern Cookbook: Stories and Recipes for Southerners and Would-be Southerners*. New York: W.W. Norton & Co., 2006.

Lewis, Edna. *The Taste of Country Cooking*. New York: Alfred A. Knopf, 1976.

————, and Scott Peacock. *The Gift of Southern Cooking: Recipes and Revelations from Two Great American Cooks*. New York: Alfred A. Knopf, 2003.

Lombard, Dr. Rudy. *Creole Feast: 15 Master Chefs of New Orleans Reveal Their Secrets*. New York: Random House, 1978.

Lundy, Ronni. *Butter Beans to Blackberries: Recipes from the Southern Garden*. New York: North Point Press/Farrar, Straus and Giroux, 1999.

————. *Shuck Beans, Stack Cake, and Honest Fried Chicken: The Heart and Soul of Southern Country Kitchens*. New York: The Atlantic Monthly Press, 1991.

McDermott, Nancie. *Southern Cakes: Sweet and Irresistible Recipes for Everyday Celebrations*. San Francisco: Chronicle Books, 2007.

Neal, Bill. *Bill Neal's Southern Cooking*. Chapel Hill, NC: The University of North Carolina Press, 1989.

———. *Biscuits, Spoonbread, and Sweet Potato Pie*. Chapel Hill, NC: The University of North Carolina Press, 1985.

Page, Linda Garland, and Eliot Wigginton. *The Foxfire Book of Appalachian Cookery*. Chapel Hill, NC: The University of North Carolina Press, 1989.

Parker, Curtis. *The Lost Art of Scratch Cooking: Recipes from the Kitchen of Mrs. Natha Adkins Parker*. Elk Grove, CA: Curtis Parker, 1997.

Puckett, Susan, ed. *The South: The Beautiful Cookbook*. San Francisco: Harper-Collins, 1996.

Robinson, Sallie Ann. *Cooking the Gullah Way: Morning, Noon, & Night*. Chapel Hill, NC: The University of North Carolina Press, 2007.

———. *Gullah Home Cooking the Daufuskie Way: Smokin' Joe Butterbeans, Ol' Fuskie Fried Crab Rice, Sticky-Bush Blackberry Dumpling, & Other Sea Island Favorites*. Chapel Hill, NC: The University of North Carolina Press, 2003.

Sanders, Dori. *Dori Sanders' Country Cooking: Recipes and Stories from the Family Farm Stand*. Chapel Hill, NC: Algonquin Books, 2003.

Smith, Bill. *Seasoned in the South*. Chapel Hill, NC: Algonquin Books, 2005.

Sohn, Mark. *Appalachian Home Cooking: History, Culture, and Recipes*. Lexington, KY: The University Press of Kentucky, 2005.

Southern Foodways Alliance. *The Spiral Bound Bible of Southern Cooking*. Augusta, GA: University of Georgia Press, 2009.

Sparks, Elizabeth Hedgecock. *North Carolina and Old Salem Cookery*. Kernersville, NC: Menu Maker, 1960. Reprint, Chapel Hill, NC: The University of North Carolina Press, 1992.

Starr, Kathy. *The Soul of Southern Cooking*. Jackson, MS: University of Mississippi Press, 1989.

Taylor, John Martin. *Hoppin' John's Low-Country Cooking*. New York: Bantam Books, 1992.

Thurman, Sue Bailey, ed. *The Historical Cookbook of the American Negro*. Washington, DC: The National Council of Negro Women, Inc., 1958. Reprint, Boston: Beacon Press, 2000.

Tillery, Carolyn Quick. *The African-American Heritage Cookbook: Traditional Recipes and Fond Remembrances from Alabama's Renowned Tuskegee Institute*. New York: Citadel Press/Kensington, 1996.

———. *A Taste of Freedom: A Cookbook with Recipes and Remembrances from The Hampton Institute*. New York: Citadel Press/Kensington, 2002.

Walter, Eugene. *Time-Life Foods of the World: American Cooking, Southern Style*. New York: Time-Life, Inc., 1971.

White, Joyce. *Brown Sugar: Soul Food Desserts from Family and Friends*. New York: HarperCollins, 2003.

———. *Soul Food: Recipes and Reflections from African American Churches*. New York: William Morrow, 1998.

Willis, Virginia. *Bon Appetit, Y'all*. Berkeley: Ten Speed Press, 2008.

Zanger, Mark H. *The American History Cookbook*. Westport, CT: Greenwood Press, 2003.

Index

Table of Equivalents

The exact equivalents in the following have been rounded for convenience.

LIQUID/DRY MEASUREMENTS

U.S.	Metric
¼ teaspoon	1.25 m.
½ teaspoon	2.5 mil.
1 teaspoon	5 millili
1 tablespoon (3 teaspoons)	15 millil
1 fluid ounce (2 tablespoons)	30 millili
¼ cup	60 millilit
⅓ cup	80 millilit
½ cup	120 millilit
1 cup	240 millilit
1 pint (2 cups)	480 millilite
1 quart (4 cups, 32 ounces)	960 milliliter
1 gallon (4 quarts)	3.84 liters
1 ounce (by weight)	28 grams
1 pound	448 grams
2.2 pounds	1 kilogram

	Celsius	Gas
250	120	½
275	140	1
300	150	2
325	160	3
350	180	4
375	190	5
400	200	6
425	220	7
450	230	8
475	240	9
500	260	10